UNCLE WILL OF WILDWOOD

UNCLE WILL
OF WILDWOOD

Nineteenth Century Life in the Bluegrass

FRANCES JEWELL McVEY
& ROBERT BERRY JEWELL

With an introduction by Thomas D. Clark
Illustrations by Robert James Foose

THE UNIVERSITY PRESS
OF KENTUCKY

Publication of this volume was made possible in part by a grant
from the National Endowment for the Humanities.

Editorial and Sales Offices: The University Press of Kentucky
663 South Limestone Street, Lexington, Kentucky 40508-4008
www.kentuckypress.com

09 08 07 06 05   5 4 3 2 1

The Library of Congress has cataloged the hardcover edition
under the following control number: 74007877

ISBN 8-8131-9147-5 (pbk.: alk. paper)

This book is printed on acid-free recycled paper meeting
the requirements of the American National Standard
for Permanence in Paper for Printed Library Materials.

Manufactured in the United States of America.

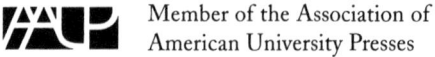 Member of the Association of
American University Presses

To Elizabeth Elliott Browne,
with the hope that when she grows up
she will enjoy reading this book as much as
her great-aunt & grandfather enjoyed writing it.

Contents

Introduction by Thomas D. Clark   ix

Author's Note   xix

1 / In a Hell of a Hurry   1

2 / Wildwood   10

3 / You Can't Get to Heaven
That Way   20

4 / Uncle Will, Sarah Eliza,
and Their Children   32

5 / They're Too Damn Good
to Sell   49

6 / Good Friends and
Clever Neighbors   73

7 / This Year—
The Beaten Biscuits   84

Introduction

ATOP THE PERIPHERY of the rolling limestone plateau just south of the Kentucky River, and on the watershed of the Salt in Mercer County is some of the finest farm land in North America. In the spring, lush pastures spread out on all sides, and grazing horses and cattle attest to the fertility of the soil. It was across the upper edge of this rich meadowland that James Harrod led his tiny band of landhunters in May 1774 to scout the territory. They saw it at its best, when both trees and shrubs were in bloom, and cane and grass competed for soil and sunlight. If there was a western eden, then Harrod and his men believed they had found it; immediately, they attempted to establish a settlement. Some of these men, Harrod included, were already familiar with the fertile soils of the Conestoga Valley in Pennsylvania, and the Kentucky plateau was even more appealing. Here was territory from which both a highly productive farm system and a distinctly rural agrarian way of life could be created.

In a remarkably brief span of time this Mercer County land evolved through the American frontier stages of corn patch and cabin settlement and expanded clearings, to furrowed fields of hemp, grain, and tobacco. The settlers who drove cattle along with their pioneering trains converted woodlands into pastures covered with thick carpets of grass. It was all but foreordained that livestock in the region would become a natural enterprise. It seemed but a brief moment on the time scale of Kentucky pioneer history between the opening of the first clearings and the development of plantations with broad fields, the raising of ample homesteads. Wildwood, the seat of the individualistic and, perhaps, eccentric Will Goddard passed through the usual stages of development. Off to one side of the present Wildwood lawn is the double log cabin that housed the first farmer on the site, shaded by the highly bastardized "Italianesque" villa, which first became a status symbol in Kentucky at mid-nineteenth century. This type of rambling house, with its high ceilings, high rise tower, and arched hallways, made almost as much appeal to affluent Kentucky countrymen as did the earlier Virginia version of Georgian colonial and Gideon Shryock's famous Greek Revival structures. Economically Wildwood was an unusually fine example of the nearly self-contained family country estate of what James Lane Allen, in Will Goddard's age, called "A Lord of the Soil." However, Wildwood produced far more than the fruits of furrow and meadow; socially it nurtured a close-knit family community, which cherished a way of life that bestowed the greatest possible freedoms on individual and group alike. Its economic security even added more than a dash of rural snobbishness, which Will Goddard showered on the denizens of Harrodsburg almost daily. To him the Kentuckian in town was either socially or economically displaced, or he was there to serve the countryman; the worthwhile man and mode of life lay beyond the village limits.

While the image of Will Goddard fixed in this book is one of full lens exposure, its fundamentals are not much blurred in the broader dimensions of social fact. All across Bluegrass Kentucky there were Will Goddards. They drew their self-confidence, social philosophy and outlook, and inordinate pride from the soil in the same way that they harvested bumper crops of corn, wheat, and hemp, or drove fat animals to market. To Will Goddard, the land gave man a sort of immortality in which human security was as inexhaustible as the limestone-laden qualities of the earth itself. It is doubtful that John Locke had Uncle Will precisely in mind in his second treatise on natural rights; nevertheless almost every Bluegrass farm gate was the entry way into a ruggedly independent domain where men much like him held individualist sway.

To a large extent these Kentucky "barons of the land" controlled the local courthouse rings; they sent their kind to the legislature, and occasionally selected a governor from their ranks. They stood ever ready to halt reforms and choke off political innovations that threatened to tilt the keels of their lives. They spoke with voices of authority in church and community councils, and they even made their wishes known in the halls of Congress. These men were patriarchs who headed families of sons and daughters to their eternal glorification. With ritualistic regularity they herded their broods into surreys and drove away to the Kentucky spas to enjoy seasons of socializing with their social equals. But whatever they did, or whatever they talked about, their minds seldom wandered far from the central theme, land.

As exciting as were the social swirls about the springs, they were not enough to absorb all the energies of the farmers and their families. After 1850, affluent Bluegrass farmers organized and sustained, somewhat after the English pattern, two of the most important agricultural and social institutions in this country. These were the livestock shows and sales, and the county fairs. In Kentucky's most exciting decade, the 1850s, these institutions came to full flower. In its characteristic rural agrarian way, the country fair, like the medieval gatherings of chivalry, pitted one farm family against another in contests of personal talents and the productivity of their respective lands. For Will Goddard the Mercer County Fair broke the day-to-day routine of farm management, if not the late summer doldrums. The rivalries renewed challenges to establish his self-esteem concerning family and Wildwood.

Wildwood was operated largely by members of the Goddard family. There were most certainly slaves, but they seem to have played a secondary role in farm operations. Anyway Wildwood was not the kind of plantation on which slaves could be used with profit. Its crop routine was largely one that required little intensive hand work, and grain and hemp were sown broadcast, which eliminated tedious row crop cultivation. Will Goddard's strong pro-southern sentiment was more a matter of emotions than reasoned political convictions or basic economic interests. He had a family background in the South, and most certainly had congress with southerners when they came to the springs during the summers. Harrodsburg at one time was a mecca for southern visitors to the famous Graham Springs. Uncle Will's antipathy for "damyankees" probably derived from the same general source. He knew few northerners, and it may well have been that the ones he did know were within the caste of peddlers and itinerant merchants.

When the crises of sectional conflict settled upon the country in 1860–1861, the Goddards, like all other Bluegrass Kentuckians, were concerned with the outcome of the crucial presidential election. Beriah Magoffin, Governor of the Commonwealth, represented the opinion of the Mercer County farmers. Public opinion of the country about Wildwood was pro-southern and soon after the firing on Fort Sumter, sons of Mercer, Anderson, and Boyle counties rode away to join southern forces. Some of them fought with John Hunt Morgan. The region was to experience a good amount of excitement in the first two years of the war. Many persons in Mercer County no doubt believed the South would be victorious. On July 12, 1862, when John Hunt Morgan galloped his flamboyant command of mounted infantrymen into Harrodsburg on his way up from Tennessee, the ladies of the town greeted his arrival with breakfast for the entire troop—a breakfast that would have done credit to Wildwood itself. The war was still a gentleman's fight, and the natives knew nothing of the grim realities of a bloody battlefield; this they were to learn before the year's end.

In early fall 1862 Kentucky became a focal center of the war as Braxton Bragg undertook to push the southern line northward toward the Ohio River. Kirby Smith had ridden and fought his way from Cumberland Gap to Lexington. Morgan's men were back in the state; so were Breckinridge and Humphrey Marshall. At nearby Shakertown the invaders raided larder and pasture on their way to meet the Yankees of Don Carlos Buell. Fortunately, Wildwood was off the main road, and few if any troops from either army were in its immediate area. But on October 3, the bloody battle of Perryville occurred within hearing of the Goddard farm. The roar of this fierce encounter spread a sense of doom across the fertile meadowland, and Uncle Will could easily have heard its message in the clear tones of cannon fire. If he had gone to Pleasant Hill during the next three days, or to Harrodsburg, he could have seen first-hand evidence of the South's up-hill fight.

However, the war came no closer to the rich and luxurious fields of Will Goddard's barony than Harrodsburg. His livestock grazed peaceably in his meadows as they had done for the past seventy years. No thieving Confederate or Yankee conscriptor laid hand on a prize pony or shoat, and more important, the Goddard family suffered no damage more serious than bruised pride and dampened hopes. Except for the general disturbance of social and economic conditions in the region, isolated Bluegrass farmsteads like Wildwood were left to nurture their even tenor of life.

Actually, the war and following aftermath of political reconstruction did little to disrupt the way of life in the Kentucky Bluegrass. In time the Confederates captured the state by getting themselves elected to key public offices. The heyday of the Bluegrass masters of rich landed estates was from 1870 to 1910. Their pastures produced more and better quality livestock. Files of yellowing stock show catalogs for the period reveal an almost feverish interest in breeding and grazing.

Hemp farmers in the late 1870s found a bumptious rival to the historic hemp industry in the new burley tobacco. The fields that had grown hemp were quickly planted to this broad-leaved newcomer, and the new American tobacco trade found a ready supply of raw materials. Every phase of farming in the Bluegrass underwent change, most of it to the good of the farmers. They not only accepted the change, but hastened it with their rivalries at fairs and stock shows. More than ever in Kentucky history the county fair became a central social and agricultural institution.

After the crucial year 1860 few southerners came upriver during the summers to take the waters at Kentucky spas and seek husbands for eligible daughters. The hotels and springs went into a decline, and the annual county fair rapidly took their place. Will Goddard and his family were good examples of this new type of socializing and serious farm competition.

The authors of this book make a point of Uncle Will's being eternally in "a hell of a hurry." He was, and so were most other Bluegrass farmers. The land was on a natural schedule, and its fertility pushed crops up fast. Planting and harvesting seasons often came close together, and in some instances, simultaneously. The seasons, too, had direct bearings on the use of time. A dry day in haying season was precious; a mowing machine breakdown could bring about the loss of a crop. Tobacco had to be cut and housed on nature's schedule; so did small grains and corn. Except for the frigidly dormant months of January and February there was no time on a farm like Wildwood when a farmer could relax his pace. Thus it was that Will Goddard's nervous system was attuned to the land, the seasons, the crops, the lambing seasons, sales days, and county fairs.

The story of Will Goddard lies somewhere between the hard facts of farming in Mercer County and family memories. Well before he made his last mad dash into Harrodsburg for a mowing machine part, Uncle Will had become a family and community legend. It is doubtful that Will Goddard made any permanent record of his activities—except for the bits of information he gave the decennial census takers, the recorded deed to Wildwood in the Mercer County Clerk's office, and his marriage record deposited with the Circuit Clerk. He nevertheless left a small army of children, grandchildren, and great-grandchildren unto the third, fourth, and even fifth generations, who have kept his memory green by repeating the stories about their eccentric and colorful forebear.

Frances Jewell McVey (1889–1945), great-grandniece of Will Goddard, and co-author of this book, was herself a legend in the Bluegrass. She grew up at Pleasant View Farm, the daughter of Asa H. and Lizzie Berry Jewell. Graduate of the Baldwin School, Bryn Mawr, Pennsylvania, 1907, and of Vassar College, 1913, she received the Master of Arts degree in English from Columbia University in 1918. Following graduation from Columbia she became an instructor in English at the University of Kentucky, and later dean of women. She served as a trustee of Vassar College, and in 1940 the University of Kentucky awarded her an honorary doctorate.

In 1923 Frances Jewell married Frank LeRond McVey, president of the university, and as the wife of the president of a struggling state university, Mrs. McVey quickly became a moving spirit both on the campus and in the state. She possessed many of her great-uncle Will Goddard's finer characteristics, and with keen social instincts and finesse she made the president's house, Maxwell Place, as hospitable as

Wildwood had been. Interestingly, Wildwood and Maxwell Place were both the bastard daughters of the same artistic parent, the "Italian Revival" style, and both had towers looking out upon azure seas that did not exist.

Between 1923 and 1942 Maxwell Place became nationally famous for its openhanded hospitality. However, Frances Jewell was far more than a gracious hostess. Indeed, she was a cultivated woman with literary talent. Like all Kentuckians she appreciated a good story, and Uncle Will's saga was tailor-made to please her sense of humor. In 1938 she and her brother Robert recorded this saga in a richly nostalgic narrative, describing one slender segment of life in another Kentucky age which now is well nigh beyond emotional recall. Uncle Will would have disowned both of them.

Like his sister, Robert Berry Jewell (1896–) went north to college, graduating from Williams College in 1918, just in time to become a naval aviation cadet in World War I. He too, despite his yankee education, embodies many of the generous qualities of his Uncle Will on Pleasant View Farm in Jessamine County. He has carried on a Goddard-Jewell tradition in trotting horse breeding and sales. Firsthand experience enabled him to keep the manuscript factually correct where farming operations were concerned. He knows realistically what it meant to Will Goddard to have a farm implement breakdown in planting and harvest times.

Together Frances McVey and Robert Jewell have produced a narrative rich in personal anecdote, and even more so in nostalgia. When one walks through the "forty-acre" high ceiling rooms of Will Goddard's brick castle and into his flower garden, along the country lane where many of the old trees still stand, silent witnesses to the past, and then looks out over the lush Bluegrass acres, he can well imagine the contents of this narrative. Who is there to doubt the central theme of this account of affluent Bluegrass country life? The window with its carefully beveled joints is still there. The old mounting block is still in place, a solid documentation of the day when courting daughters seated themselves gracefully in side-saddles and rode off with prospective husbands. There survives, however, no tangible evidence of a forty-five pound watermelon—yet, with the master's damned and determined will, the mighty strength of his land, and the ingenuity of his husbandry, who knows?

Thomas D. Clark

Author's Note

WHEN MY SISTER, Frances Jewell McVey, and I wrote this narrative in the late thirties, Uncle Will's era did not seem very distant, and we supposed that what we had written was of interest only to our family and the friends and neighbors who had known Uncle Will. But now, as we approach the two-hundredth anniversary of the settlement in the Great Meadow, some of those concerned with the celebration have convinced me that it is appropriate to introduce Uncle Will and his time to the 1970s.

This book is not "history" as scholars would have it. Frances and I did it mainly for fun, and we did not worry much about technicalities. For those readers who may be puzzled by our pronouns, let me explain that sometimes "I" means Frances and sometimes it means Bob. I might be hard put today to say which of us wrote a particular paragraph. The stories we tell were told to us by our mother and father, our uncles and aunts, and there may be errors in time, location, and names, for which I apologize. As I look back, I am especially grateful to Rebel Goddard and Ina Watkins, who gave us so much information about their father.

Much of what Frances and I tell about here has vanished, but Wildwood has not. It is still a prosperous farm, and the house Uncle Will built is still beautifully kept by a couple who make their neighbors welcome just as Uncle Will and Aunt Sally did. They have been most gracious to all concerned in the making of this book. Thanks in part to them, the illustrations by Robert James Foose are not just imaginings, but are based on a study of the house and of old photographs of it and of the leading characters in our story.

My sincere thanks and appreciation go to Dr. Thomas D. Clark and to my cousin, Betty Walsh Morris, for their help in resurrecting this book. I hope it will be received in the spirit in which it was written, and that you, the reader, will enjoy this brief account of the people who lived in an innocent, rollicking, bygone day.

ROBERT BERRY JEWELL
August 5, 1974

UNCLE WILL OF WILDWOOD

1

IN A HELL
OF A HURRY

My RECOLLECTION of mother's great-uncle W. W. Goddard is a cross between a hurricane and an electric fan, a whoosh and a holler in a white linen suit, carrying a long buggy whip—and in one hell of a hurry.

I remember Uncle Will mostly as he was in the summertimes, given to wearing white suits and dusters and broadbrimmed white felt hats. He was a short, stocky, extremely muscular man, about 5'7", and he kept himself in top physical trim at all times. He was *always* rushing, at a rapid gait on foot, at a gallop in a buckboard, or riding Black Joe in a dead run. He had so much to do and so little time to do it! Everybody else at Wildwood—except his Sarah Eliza, who was perfect—was so goddam lackadaisical. "Those boys and those darkies are ornery and no 'count," he'd declare. "*Somebody* around here has got to be on the move if anything's to get done!" The damn farm hands just wouldn't use their heads. And besides that, the farm implements were always breaking. If those mowers had been made in the South, he'd say, they'd be made right and stand up. Might as well have come from a foreign country as from the North. Damyankees couldn't do anything right, and the way those good-for-nothing hands could break up the farm implements just proved it. Was a man ever as busy or in such a hurry, with so much to do? He'd mutter and explode on his way home from Harrodsburg, his buckboard careening from side to side.

On this particular day Uncle Will had had a run-in with the law, and as a consequence he was driving Black Joe even faster than usual. Black Joe loved to run, and Uncle Will loved to urge the little black stallion on. Naturally, he could not be bothered by the traffic regulations that were beginning to be enforced in the 1890s, and of course, in his day, no signal lights were present to harass him. But the tollgates exasperated him beyond measure. Since Uncle Will owned stock in most of the turnpikes of Mercer County, and in many of the neighboring counties as well, he and his family did not have to pay toll. He always gave the Rebel yell in plenty of time for the tollgate keeper or his wife to raise the long locust pole so that Black Joe would not be slowed up on his way. Woe unto keeper and pole if Uncle Will had to wait!

"By god, Asa," Uncle Will used to tell my father, "Black Joe is smarter than most people." Reb, Uncle Will's second son, once said that in his father's estimation, a lady held first place, a horse second, and a man and dog tied for third—with a little preference for the dog. But Uncle Will was right about Black Joe—he *was* smart; he was also quick, independent, and tough, all qualities that appealed to Uncle Will. An understanding certainly existed between those two. Both were in a continual hurry, and both were intolerant of what they saw as the stupidity, indolence, and false pride of others. Although Black Joe did not have any pedigree to brag about, he had as good a stall as the famous stallions of Wildwood, Sumpter Denmark or Red Leaf. He was never allowed to go hungry or thirsty, and when he became too old to pull Uncle Will at a gallop, he was turned out in the pasture "to rest for awhile."

"Black Joe just needs a rest, Glave," Uncle Will explained to his eldest son. "He's not through by any means. That little stallion is tough; he'll come back all right. After he rests awhile, I'll take him up again, and he'll be as fit as ever."

The "while" was prolonged indefinitely, but Uncle Will declared: "No, by god, Black Joe's not pensioned; he's just having a short rest."

Meanwhile, other horses carried Uncle Will down the Avenue—at a gallop—and pulled him in the buckboard into Harrodsburg. I suspect that some of these were even faster than Black Joe; but Uncle Will was lonesome without the little black stallion.

"No, I'm not sentimental. Joe's all right. I'm just giving him a rest so he'll be better and carry me faster this fall."

But on this hot July day it was Black Joe who shared Uncle Will's encounter with the minions of the law.

The three miles to Harrodsburg were over a good level road with few turns, a situation for which people who lived along the road were duly thankful. When it came to making a sharp turn in a buckboard, Uncle Will was an artist. That wagon would lean so far to one side it had two wheels off the road, and everybody—except, of course, for Uncle Will—just *knew* that it would capsize. A sure bet that Mr. Goddard wouldn't make it this time! But he always did. His technique was beautiful. He'd stand up, balance on one foot, and lean just enough to the upraised side to keep the buckboard from going over. Then he'd rapidly shift his weight to the other foot in order to right it. Uncle Will knew just how to do the trick and he loved it. I can see him now, like a good sailor keeping his boat on an even keel in a stormy sea, Uncle Will taking the curves, the tails of his linen duster like rudders flying in the breeze. It was a sight to admire. But the toll in cats, dogs, and pigs was considerable. Nothing was safe that got in the way when Uncle Will and Black Joe took the turns.

3

In Harrodsburg, there was a sharp right-angled corner leading onto Main Street—a beautiful turn: a slight drop, the corner, and then straight up a hill. How was a man to resist? Uncle Will habitually gave this turn all he had. But he paid for it. He was always recompensing someone for the dogs, cats, and occasional shoats that had somehow become involved in his artistic manipulation of the Lexington Avenue–Main Street corner. George Morgan paid for it too. He *lived* on that corner, and already he'd lost two cats, a Plymouth Rock hen, a shoat, and a duck to the progress of that stallion and the little man in the linen duster navigating the buckboard.

Uncle Will was genuinely sorry when he and Black Joe ran over George Morgan's hound bitch. Uncle Will liked hound dogs; he hoped that someday he would have the time to hunt them. In fact, nothing stirred his blood more than to sit around a fire and hear the hounds afar off "giving mouth." Now Ike Gaither's bitch would be leading the pack, and then Tom Coleman's Alexander would take the lead. And none of those hounds would ever catch a thing. That wiley fox always seemed to run in a wide circle—and actually *wait* for the dogs if they happened to hit a false trail. Then too, the fox only ran until it got tired, and then it simply went back to its den. It was great sport, though, for each fox hunter knew his own dog's mouth. No hunter ever spoke of his dog's voice or bark or howl; he always said his dog was "giving mouth." And the dogs, how they loved the hunt! They'd run all night led on by that sly red-coated animal; and apparently, the fox was having a lot of fun itself!

Why in *hell* did George Morgan's bitch have to be crossing the street at the Harrodsburg corner just when he and Black Joe were making that priceless turn? It really was a shame! She had whelped only a few days before. She wasn't hurt or anything, but the poor thing was frightened half to death.

4

Immediately Uncle Will hunted up George Morgan and offered to pay him for any damages. But George refused.

"Will Goddard, I don't want your money. No harm's done this time. But you really ought to come into town more slowly."

"You're goddamn right," agreed Uncle Will, "but I'm always in such a hell of a hurry."

The truth was that George Morgan's patience was getting a trifle threadbare. He liked Will Goddard because Will was a square shooter, with plenty of guts, and a man of his word. But George was also pretty fond of his own livestock. Moreover he thought Will Goddard needed a lesson, and he was not alone in his peeve.

Uncle Will not only came into town like a bat out of hell. When he reached the store or office where he had business to attend to he simply jumped out of the buckboard, leaving Black Joe to wander at will up and down the street. What usually resulted was that Black Joe would manage to lock the wheels of the buckboard into the wheels of some other buggy, thereby impeding traffic on that side of the street and obliging whoever owned the other vehicle to wait for Uncle Will's return so that together they could disengage their buggies. Granted, nobody ever had to wait long on Mr. W. W. Goddard; nonetheless he and Black Joe were trying in this particular. Something really had to be done about it. Hints and suggestions had been of no avail: a lesson would have to be taught him.

Unfortunately for Uncle Will, the next day he ran down a guinea hen that belonged across the street from George Morgan. I think that guinea was the last straw; the cumulative effect of Black Joe and Uncle Will's pride in making the turn at full speed on two wheels now brought about definite action.

At the meeting of the Town Council on Tuesday night, an ordinance was passed forbidding anyone to come into Harrodsburg at an excessive and reckless rate of speed; forbidding anyone to drive on the lefthand side of the street; and forbidding anyone to leave his horse untied and untended in the town. Further, anyone found violating this ordinance would be fined $10.00.

Now this ordinance had not come right out and mentioned W. W. Goddard by name, but it might as well have because it was meant for him and for him alone. The city fathers had gone home from the council meeting in a solemn frame of mind. This ordinance was no joke. As much as they hated doing it, they had passed the ordinance unanimously. They were all friends, neighbors, or relatives of W. W. Goddard, and they'd done this really for his own good. What if he ran over somebody and killed him? He'd never get over it.

Actually, Uncle Will was not very likely to run over anybody because everybody knew the corner and everybody knew Uncle Will and Black Joe. No one ever crossed before taking a good look both ways. Children were warned from their first steps to look out for the approaching hurricane of Uncle Will.

On Wednesday morning, bright and early, Tom Coleman rode over to Wildwood just as Uncle Will was coming in from his morning inspection of the farm. Tom told him of the ordinance passed the night before and tried to warn him of the result of violation.

"It's a damn good idea, Tom," Uncle Will asserted. "I'm always for anything that will cut down on accidents. Too much reckless driving going on these days, and too many people driving who don't know how to drive."

Uncle Will meant what he said. He was quite unaware of his own misdemeanors and hardly suspected that the ordinance had been written for him. What did recklessness have to do with Black Joe and that turn? Dammit, he was a good driver.

That same morning the pitman rod in the mower was broken ("some more of Reb's carelessness") and Pete, one of the hands, was sent to hitch Black Joe to the buckboard so that Uncle Will could go to town for the rod.

The clover had to be cut, the weather was dry, and although there probably wouldn't be any rain until the moon changed, there was no time to be lost. Uncle Will didn't even stop to put on his linen duster—he jumped into the buckboard and was gone. Somehow Black Joe sensed the need for haste; he just seemed to *know* that putting up clover hay was a ticklish job. The hay would be spoiled by rain, and you couldn't let it stand too long before cutting it either. There was a time to cut hay and that time was now! So they were off to Harrodsburg—at an even faster clip than usual.

On the way he passed Tom Coleman, who was returning home, leisurely riding his horse in a walk. Uncle Will shouted at him as he went by in a cloud of dust. Tom shook his head; he knew what was going to happen.

Uncle Will made a particularly fine turn onto Main Street that morning and he jumped from the buckboard in front of Grant Vivion's hardware store. Black Joe was in the process of wandering away to the other side of the street, and Uncle Will was just entering the store when the town marshal touched him on the shoulder. Only then did Uncle Will remember the ordinance.

Tom Coleman had told him about the fine for driving too fast and not fastening your horse to the hitching post. In fact, he remembered thinking that Black Joe wouldn't like being tied up, for he had never been hitched in all the years they'd been coming to town.

The marshal didn't have to tell him what he wanted. Uncle Will already knew, and it was too late to do anything about it. Without a word of objection he followed the marshal into the courthouse and stood before the magistrate. Slowly and significantly, the magistrate read the ordinance. Uncle Will hadn't any time to listen to the damn thing, but for once in his life he held his temper and his tongue.

8

The magistrate asked him if he had anything to say. Uncle Will shook his head. All he wanted to do was get back to Wildwood as quickly as possible. He would take his medicine.

But the magistrate felt called upon to make a speech.

"Mr. Goddard, you are a fine man, a reasonable man, and I hate to do this. It is my duty; otherwise I should never do it. I know that you, Mr. Goddard, did not intentionally break this law. But the wording of the ordinance is clear. Moreover, Mr. Coleman was commissioned to explain the ordinance to you in detail in order that you would know about it and conduct yourself accordingly. What is more you have not protested your innocence. You have indicated that you have nothing to say for yourself."

Uncle Will stood first on one foot and then on the other in his anxiety to be through with the matter. The magistrate went on.

"Mr. Goddard, you can see for yourself just why these steps had to be taken," he droned unctuously. "I know that you are a just man, a widely respected man. I did not make this law, you understand. But it is my duty, Mr. Goddard, and I hate to do it, you must know; but it is my duty to fine you $10.00."

It seemed to Uncle Will that the magistrate had been going on all day. He pulled his wallet from his hip pocket, took out a twenty, tossed it on the magistrate's desk, and started for the door. He was in a hell of a hurry. By this time Black Joe had probably wandered up to Dr. Price's plum tree; that horse just *loved* plum leaves—and plums too. Dr. Price had never seemed very pleased to have Black Joe visit his plum tree.

"Mr. Goddard!" the magistrate called as Uncle Will got to the door. "Don't you want your change? You gave me a twenty, and the fine was only $10.00."

"I know very well that fine is $10.00," snapped Uncle Will. "You just *keep* that other ten because, by god, I'm going out of Harrodsburg the same way I came in!"

9

2

WILDWOOD

To the northeast and southwest of Harrodsburg the land sloped gently to the Kentucky River. The land was very fertile; gradual slopes gave it drainage, and the springs gushing from the understratum of limestone rock made for healthy livestock.

As a natural consequence of such conditions, there grew up a neighborhood of prosperous farmers and stock breeders who had come to live on the site of what was the Great Meadow. These men were first of all good farmers; some were horsebreeders; some specialized in cattle or sheep or hogs. But they all lived well. Their wives had good driving horses and buggies. Each of the most prosperous had a team and a coachman who was also gardener and butler, or when the harvest was on, just another hand.

Since each family in the neighborhood had from one to maybe ten good driving horses, racing home from church or Saturday shopping became inevitable. If a man had a horse that could outrace the other horses in the neighborhood, he'd send it to be professionally trained and raced. All the county fairs had harness races, and the meeting held at the Trotting Track in Lexington every fall was a national event.

All in all, it was a leisurely existence (though Uncle Will himself did not know the meaning of the word *leisure*). Fox hunting and cock fighting were common, and every gentleman had his barrel of whiskey in the cellar. Social life centered in the neighborhood. A trip to Lexington, Louisville, or Cincinnati was an occasion in the 1890s; and when a visit was made away from home, it lasted for several weeks or months.

In Uncle Will's day, Harrodsburg and Mercer County were a pleasant and comfortable spot, much as they are today, inhabited by gentle folk who lived graciously, but at times violently. The considerable wealth of the county was built on hemp, tobacco, and livestock; it had been drawn from the fertile soil, once tilled by slaves, and later, after the Emancipation Proclamation, by Negroes who would not leave their homes and masters, and by tenant farmers.

Uncle Will never doubted that this part of the Bluegrass region was God's Country. It was a good place to live; to raise his family of nine children; to hate those damyankees; and to surround himself with his broad acres, his shorthorn cattle, and his saddle horses. The county was known throughout the United States for the production of fast trotters and thoroughbreds, fine saddle horses, and prizewinning shorthorn cattle. Some of the finest horses and cattle in the world were bred and owned in Mercer County.

No king could have been prouder of his castle than Uncle Will was of Wildwood. Wildwood was the best farm a man could own, he'd declare firmly; the shorthorn cattle were the finest of the breed; Sumpter Denmark was, by god, the best saddle horse sire in the world; those corner acres raised the finest damn tobacco anywhere; Sarah Eliza was the best wife a man ever had; and those nine children were, without a doubt, the smartest and handsomest in the whole South. (The North was another country altogether; it might as well have been the Congo for all it counted in Uncle Will's reckoning.) When my father asked him one day how it was that so much perfection could have fallen to the lot of one man, Uncle Will replied earnestly, "By god, Asa, I'm not lying; I think they *are* the best."

Uncle Will was thirty-nine years old when he married Sarah Eliza Glave and brought her from Cynthiana to live at Wildwood. He had built her a house from walnut logs cut on the place. Later, he built the large red brick house with big rooms, high ceilings, and a tower topping the third floor. When the children were older, the boys of the family moved into the log house, and it was always referred to as the cottage.

Uncle Will's room was on the first floor of the big house where the windows extended to the floor, opening out onto the porch. And that was the way Uncle Will went into those rooms—through the windows. Who had time to fool with doors and entrance halls? If the window was down, Uncle Will knocked the glass out and kept on going. He had too damn much to do to let a panel of glass get in his way.

The barns and other outbuildings were made of logs covered with weatherboarding and always kept in good condition. Large paddocks surrounded the one-stall barns that housed the stallion, Sumpter Denmark; the jack, Jack Spann; and the bull, King of Sharon.

Black locust, walnut, ash, tulip poplar, elm, and oak trees were in abundance. From the house an avenue of sugar maple trees led to the road, and in addition to the large trees native to Central Kentucky, Uncle Will had set out on his estate hemlocks, lindens, willows, honey lindens, gingkos, catalpas, mountain ash, and many others. Three hammocks were stretched out between the trees on the lawn, and although no one ever saw Uncle Will in a hammock, he had them put up without fail every spring. From the limb of a large oak tree there hung a rope swing, and I remember how the boys (girls too, if Uncle Will was not looking) used to pump and pump and get the seat of the swing almost perpendicular to the ground before they'd "let the cat die."

On the lawn there were hickory chairs and a large

hickory table used primarily as an accouterment for the rite of slicing watermelons. Black and coral honeysuckle vines climbed up trellises and over stumps. Under one parlor window there grew a luxuriant bed of lilies of the valley; under another the August lilies, whose leaves we used for plates and hats as children. In front of the house, on either side of a brick walk leading down to the stone horse-block, stood huge tubs of oleanders, crepe myrtles, cape jasmines, pomegranates, lemon verbenas, and fuchsias. These were brought out in the spring when the danger of frost was past, and returned to the cellar before the first frost in the fall. The containers were so large and the plants so heavy that four men were assigned to the task.

About three hundred feet from the house, a brick springhouse had been built over a flowing spring. Here in the dairy, milk and butter stayed cool and sweet. Here too, when the summer came, Uncle Will stored those huge delicious watermelons. There were never such watermelons as Uncle Will's—always striped, never solid green.

To the south, along the side of the dining room, lay a flower garden, and one could enter it by means of those long windows that reached to the floor. This half acre of color was Sarah Eliza's special delight, and the workmen were never too busy to help her make that garden one to be remembered. Roses, lemon lilies, poppies, Madonna lilies, peonies, narcissi, and iris bloomed in profusion. Later in the spring blue veronica and yellow coreopsis vied with purple campanulas, red sweet williams, and varicolored cinnamon pinks. They all blossomed riotously, for the sheer joy of living. Song sparrows and cardinals sang for them by morning, and the mocking birds came to show off in the moonlight, imitating the songs of the day. Honeysuckle perfumed the air in early summer; and migonette, bleeding heart, snapdragons, columbine, China asters, foxgloves, and chrysanthemums all bloomed in their accustomed times to carry the pageant of color well into autumn. Holly-hocks bordered the driveway; and against the white picket fence that enclosed the garden, the solemn sun-flowers stood, like sentries with a thousand eyes, following the July sun.

Near Sarah Eliza's bedroom Uncle Will had built a pit with a glass over the top as a kind of greenhouse; here grew the Maréchal Neil rose for which Mrs. Goddard and Wildwood were famous. Visitors to Harrodsburg were often brought out to see the yellow rose, and perhaps in the process to get a glimpse of Mr. Goddard. In spite of the respect in which he was held, Uncle Will was somewhat of a curiosity to many people, and his sayings and philosophy were quoted all over the state. As for the squire of Wildwood himself, he was not at all surprised that everyone wanted to see "the most beautiful yellow rose, the best livestock, and the finest tobacco in the world."

On one side of the flower garden he had planted an orchard with rows of cherry, plum, pear, apple, peach, and crabapple trees. On the other side lay the vegetable garden filled with all *kinds* of vegetables, from a row of rhubarb at one end to the asparagus bed at the other. All around the garden there were currant, gooseberry, and raspberry bushes, and a long strawberry patch to one side. A grape arbor led from the garden to the house, and here, in July and August, the vines were bent under huge bunches of purple, red, and white grapes.

The rich farm land with its fields of hemp, tobacco, wheat, corn, rye, oats, clover, and tree-studded bluegrass pastures for the livestock rolled away from the house and yard and gardens in undulating beauty. And through this peaceful countryside Uncle Will dashed in a gallop on his stud pony Black Joe.

He enjoyed his farm, and he enjoyed showing his prize stock to his friends. I often wondered how he had time to enjoy *anything*, but I guess he took his pleasures on the wing. He positively reveled in his early morning pre-breakfast rides over the 325 acres and outer boundaries of his farm.

Over the mantelpiece in the large parlor at Wildwood hung an oil painting of three fat cows on toothpick legs, knee-deep in bluegrass, against a background of the house at Wildwood. Uncle Will always showed this picture to his guests. First he'd give them the pedigree of the strange looking animals, and say, "Those are the cows I sold Abe Renick for $900 apiece." Then he never failed to add, "The artist who painted the picture never took a lesson in her life." I was never able to determine just how firmly he'd planted his tongue in his cheek when he made this remark.

Uncle Will did permit himself a bit of leisure at Wildwood on Sundays, and of course he enjoyed the activities there at all times. He delighted in peoples' reactions to the beauties of Wildwood, the lovely old garden beyond his and Sarah Eliza's bedroom, the peafowls, the crepe myrtles, and the Maréchal Neil roses. He wanted all of his friends to come—and he wanted them all to get plenty to eat! Even on the hottest days, one could find a gentle breeze in the deep shade of the big trees on the lawn. It was so easy to rest and sleep and dream at Wildwood—when Uncle Will was away from home.

Wildwood was never without company. The nine children had their friends come to visit them; nieces and nephews and cousins came to spend the whole summer; relatives and friends dropped in to stay the night, to spend the day, to visit for several days—or weeks.

On Sunday afternoons in August, our family would drive the sixteen miles from Pleasant View to Wildwood. Crowds of people would be gathered in the front yard. These Sunday afternoon assemblies had been going on for years, and by the time I entered the feast, the older children had married. Some of them came with their husbands and wives and children to spend weeks or months at Wildwood. The other families drove out every Sunday afternoon—unless they were already there spending the entire day.

Young gentlemen in no-top buggies or vehicles with high stepping horses, from Harrodsburg and other towns within driving range, came to call on the Goddard girls and their visitors. They were often accompanied by young ladies who had ostensibly come to see the girls but hoped to garner a few words and flirtatious looks from the Goddard boys. Older people drove in buggies and surreys and carriages. The horses were hitched to the trees at the sides of the house.

Chairs were brought out for all the ladies, and Uncle Will ordered the boys and young men to bring up the watermelons from the springhouse. I delighted in going to the springhouse with the big boys and selecting the watermelons. Salt in big open saltcellars, plates, forks, and a huge kitchen knife were brought from the house by Ina and Rea, the two young daughters of the house.

The cutting of the watermelons was a ritual of which Uncle Will was high priest. He carefully surveyed the watermelons before him and always chose the largest. "This watermelon weighs forty-five pounds, and I have been saving it for this Sunday afternoon. By god, it's the biggest watermelon I ever grew!"

He'd stick a knife into the middle of the melon and begin cutting an inch-square piece. "I know it's good, but anyway I'd better plug it," he'd say, flourishing the luscious sample on his butcher knife. He'd then insert the knife in the hole he'd made by plugging and cut the melon across. Invariably, it fell apart with that cracking sound that means an excellent melon. He'd cut the halves lengthwise into two pieces and cut each person a half a round three inches thick. The pieces were so large that they kept sliding from the plates. The ladies would beg him to cut their pieces in two because they really could not eat so much. And he'd comply, reluctantly, telling them to come back for more.

17

While all were eating, Uncle Will would ask Ina to bring him the watermelon seed jar. In solemn rite he'd go from guest to guest gathering up the seeds. He always saved the seeds from the best melons for next year's planting, and to give to neighbors and friends. But somehow, none of them, even with Uncle Will's selected seed, ever succeeded in equaling the Wildwood watermelons.

3

YOU CAN'T GET TO HEAVEN THAT WAY

Uncle Will belonged to no church for reasons that seemed convincing to him. There were just too many damn hypocrites in the churches, he said. He did like the Shakers, however; they lived only three miles or so from Wildwood at Pleasant Hill, and Uncle Will sometimes traded shorthorns with them. Brother Ephriam, Brother James Settle, and Dr. Pennybaker were always delighted to see him arriving in a cloud of dust, the tails of his duster flying in the breeze and Black Joe galloping.

Uncle Will liked the Shakers because they were energetic, thrifty, and good judges of livestock, and he had respect for their sincere convictions on most matters. But their pacifism made his blood boil. "Why didn't they get fighting-mad at the damyankees?" Moreover, when they objected to John Hunt Morgan's taking their horses during the Civil War his patience was at an end. "As for *me*," Uncle Will ejaculated, "Morgan and his men can have every goddamn horse at Wildwood and all the chickens and pigs thrown in."

There were four classes of people whom Uncle Will could not abide: hypocrites, liars, damyankees, and drunkards. And I'll have to grant him, if Uncle Will was anything at all, he was none of the four. What he did the whole world could see, and if he thought it was right, the whole world could "like it or lump it"; he didn't give a damn. He didn't "by god, believe in Sunday praying and Saturday drinking and Friday lying and Thursday cheating." He was just before he was generous. He was loyal, and really quite kind; he could never refuse a request for food or money. But when it came to lying, drunkenness, and hypocrisy, his intolerance knew no bounds. He was an ardent prohibitionist (though it must be allowed that he kept a decanter of whiskey on the mantelpiece—for its medicinal quality). But drunkenness he abhorred. Woe betide the callers who had whiskey on their breaths when they came to see him on business!

One day, as Uncle Will was going into the front door at the Phoenix Hotel in Lexington, a young man bumped into him and pushed him aside. That was enough for Mr. Goddard. He hauled off and knocked the man down the steps into the street—and then followed right behind him, eyes blazing, buggy whip clutched in his left hand, linen duster flying in the breeze. A friend rushed up to ask what had happened.

"He pushed me aside as I went through the door up there," said Uncle Will, pointing with his whip to the door at the head of the steps, "and *no one* shoves W. W. Goddard around." The friend leaned over the man lying on the street and said, "Why, Mr. Goddard, he's only drunk."

"Well, dammit then, I'll hit the son of a bitch again—once for pushing me aside and once for being drunk!"

This intense hatred of whiskey may have accounted in part for his admiration of William Jennings Bryan, who was not only a hero to Uncle Will but a close personal friend. Uncle Will believed in Bryan and supported him with all enthusiasm for the presidency in 1896. He never failed to show visitors the photograph taken of Mr. Bryan holding one of the Goddard grand-children in front of Wildwood.

Sarah Eliza was pleased that her husband was inter-ested in Mr. Bryan—perhaps his influence would bring Mr. Goddard into the church. Her own affiliation with the Methodist Church had begun soon after her mar-riage to Uncle Will.

As far as Uncle Will was concerned, everything Sarah Eliza did was perfect. If she had wanted to embrace cannibalism, I'm sure it would have been okay with him. She was a remarkable woman, as gentle and as calm as Uncle Will was turbulent. A quiet, "Now, Mr. Goddard," (and of course in those days a lady always addressed her husband as "Mr.") was enough to settle him. He adored her and wanted her to have everything her heart desired. I've never seen a better balance wheel for any man than Sarah Eliza was for Uncle Will. No matter how he'd rave and charge and swear about some matter, she never changed her expression, not even by a flicker of an eyelid. She knew how to carry her point in a quiet, gentle way. And carry it she did. She knew her man. With a woman of less stature he would never have been the man he was.

So if Sarah Eliza wanted to be baptized in the Meth-odist Church, by god, she would! And he himself would take her to church to do it. He got out the Prince Albert coat he'd had made when Bob Berry married, and had Red Leaf hitched up to the New Mawer buggy: he was going to take her in style! That buggy simply shone, Red Leaf was black as an eel and handsome as Pegasus, Sarah Eliza had on a new dress, and Uncle Will was dressed within an inch of his life.

When they got to the church, Uncle Will helped Aunt Sally out of the buggy and told her to wait for him while he took Red Leaf to the livery stable across the street. She thought sure that Uncle Will would walk her to the church door and leave, for she had never been able to get him inside of a church. But Uncle Will went on in.

He put his grey felt broadbrimmed hat in the back pew, and they continued down the aisle, he and Sarah Eliza. Every minute she thought he'd stop in a pew and let her go on alone. When they got to the front pew she was sure that he'd sit there. Not Uncle Will! He marched like a good soldier right up to the preacher and there he stood while his Sarah Eliza was solemnly and reverently baptized. When all was over, she took her husband's arm and they walked back down the aisle together and out of the church.

The congregation was amazed. The first time Mr. Goddard had ever been in church! As he entered, there were nudgings and whisperings that *he* was going to be baptized as well. And, of course, the preacher did not know what to make of the proceedings. He was not surprised, however, because he had learned that Mr. Goddard was a most unpredictable man.

A few days later, one of the congregation asked Uncle Will what he meant by coming in and standing by Mrs. Goddard while she was being baptized. "It was rather unconventional," he said. Uncle Will did not know the meaning of the word; at least he never practiced conventionality just to be practicing it. "Well," said Uncle Will, "Sarah Eliza wanted to be baptized, and I wanted her to be baptized, and I intended on being close at hand to see that it was done *right*. No halfway measures for *my* wife! If I had anything to say about it, she was going to have the best damn baptism ever performed in Mercer County."

That was the first time Uncle Will ever went to church in Harrodsburg. The last was a number of years later.

At this time, a very celebrated missionary was holding a protracted meeting; all Harrodsburg was discussing the preacher, the singing, and the terrible needs of the heathen in the Belgian Congo. The girls went every night with their beaux. The boys hitched up their buggies and took their best girls. In those days nothing

was more conducive to courting than a moonlit night and a horse and buggy on the way home from a good hellfire and damnation sermon—not to mention a mournful missionary appeal. Both tended to wake up dormant emotions!

Finally, Papa himself decided to go. The girls claimed they had persuaded him; the boys knew *they* hadn't. Sarah Eliza said nothing. But she hummed a little tune now and again. So they went to the revival. The deacons were a little in awe as they shook hands with Mr. Goddard, but the preacher smiled. He had been informed by the church grapevine that a brand was being plucked from the fire. It was a religious triumph to get Mr. Goddard to church, and many a palm leaf fan hid the whispers of Mrs. Cecil to Mrs. Riker and of Mrs. Riker to Mrs. Curry in the pew ahead.

Despite a perceptible tension, everything tended to go rather smoothly—that is, until the collection was taken. The deacons took up the offerings in little dark red velvet bags that were attached to long black walnut sticks. That way a deacon could stand at the edge of the pew and pass the bag to the other end without letting go of the handle. Uncle Will happened to be sitting next to the aisle, and as the bag passed by, he put in a quarter; the bag moved on to the other end of the pew and was drawn back. But as the deacon turned to the next pew, Uncle Will caught him by the coattails. "Hold on," he said loudly, drawing out a dollar bill from his wallet, "I've put a quarter in the collection bag for the heathen in the Belgian Congo; now here's a dollar to take that quarter where it's going!"

During Uncle Will's later days there lived a locally famous Negro preacher by the name of Peter. On Sunday mornings, Peter's pulpit was the front of the Phoenix Hotel in Lexington. There he'd expound the scriptures to the edification and sometimes the amusement of his various listeners. When he preached on "It's a damn hot day," or "Hell's a half-mile from Lexington," his oratory would wane and rise according to the amount of gin Peter had been able to acquire that morning. I think that probably his best sermon was entitled, "Down where the columbine twineth and the whangdoodle calleth to his mate." Peter's sermons were always graphic and his delivery was picturesque. In the sermon on the damn hot day, which he always preached when the thermometer was at its highest, he would foretell the way it was going to be for sinners on the Judgment Day. On that day all who were not saved would be damned, and it would indeed be a damn hot day for *them!*

During the harvest season it was not an uncommon practice for farmers wishing to keep the Negroes late in order to finish up the threshing or hay cutting to get Peter to hold a service after the work was all done. Part of Peter's job would be to exhort the hands to keep on working: "When you get through, I'se goin' to preach 'Hell's a half-mile from Lexington.' " Peter's customary price for this service was a bottle of gin, but considering Uncle Will's feelings about liquor, other arrangements probably were made when he preached to the hands at Wildwood.

One of Peter's sermons was "Watch that snake." The Devil was a snake that had to be watched. With much exhortation and recital of sins, Peter would suddenly rise on his toes, thrust his arms forward, and point quickly to the ground yelling, "Watch that snake!" Every five or six sentences were brought to a climax by the same cry, and the repetition was enough to cast a kind of spell over a congregation; they'd actually *look* for that snake every time Peter rose up and said "Watch!"

The revivals that Peter conducted often lasted as long as six weeks. But there was one he held in Harrodsburg that had gone well over the promised time. The owner of the land on which Peter was holding this revival had repeatedly asked him to bring his meeting to a close, but the preacher just kept putting off the ending. Business was good; the Negroes had money from their harvesting labors, and every night converts and backsliders came up to confess their sins.

Thursday was to be a big night. Peter's text was "Watch that snake." All the congregation had heard the same sermon many times, but the flow of words, the fear of impending doom, and Peter's histrionics fascinated them. When Peter had taken on a pint or so of gin, the sermon began. The night was hot, the sweating was copious—and the landowner was exasperated. His patience was at an end. That night he brought up a Jersey bull with the intention of putting him in the field next to the revival tent. He figured he'd wait for Peter and his congregation to get warmed up, induce the bull to come to the tent opening, and give them all such a scare that the meeting would break up for good.

Peter was in top form; the gin was taking hold, the sweat was pouring, and the words were flowing. "You Niggers go dancin' roun' on Sat'day night and you drinks whiskey and you shoots craps: Watch that snake!" Again and again, he enumerated their wrongdoings, and then rose to his toes for the climax. Arms outstretched, he was all set to deliver his warning, when he glanced toward the rear of the tent. There it was: the Jersey bull, its nostrils dilated, eyes shining, feet pawing the ground! Peter didn't miss a beat. "Watch that snake!" he cried, "—and for god's sake watch that *bull!*" With that parting admonition, he was off the pulpit and out of the tent.

Wildwood itself played host to a revival one night, although I suspect that Uncle Will was caught a little off guard by the request. He had stopped on the turnpike on his way home from Harrodsburg to make a minor repair to the fence, when he was approached by a large Negro in a "magnolious" Prince Albert coat and Abraham Lincolnesque silk hat. Uncle Will knew the man's

profession immediately, of course. He might have mistaken a gambler for an undertaker, by god, but a Negro preacher—never looked like anything but a Negro preacher.

This particular preacher was very upset about the way some of the Harrodsburg Negroes were behaving. "They needs a good revivin'," he declared, "and I'se just the man can do it!" If Mr. Goddard would allow him, he wanted to pitch his tent in the ash grove on the other side of the road from the house and put on a *real* revival. After much persuasion, Uncle Will finally consented, but all the way home and all that morning he worried about it. What if some sort of trouble developed? Still, he had given the preacher his permission, and "by god, I'm a man of my word."

After supper that night, Uncle Will mounted Black Joe and started down to see how preparations for the revival were coming along. Along the way he was delayed for about an hour, and when he got to the ash grove, the meeting was in full swing. The congregation was in mid-song, and Uncle Will listened with pleasure—he liked music, and these spirituals were really good! When he drew close to the tent, the preacher, resplendent in his Prince Albert, was in a lather of perspiration. The night was warm, and he was good and hot and ready to give his congregation the works.

"My sermon tonight will be on the Kingdom of Heaven," he intoned, and cleared his throat magnificently. "First, what *is* the Kingdom of Heaven? The Kingdom of Heaven is a Mysterious Mystery of Mystified Mysteries. That's what the Kingdom of Heaven is!" Having cleared up that little matter of definition, the preacher proceeded with his sermon.

When Uncle Will got home that night he said to Sarah Eliza: "I've learned something today, something new. I now know the proper definition of farming: it is a Mysterious Mystery of Mystified Mysteries!"

One afternoon, Uncle Will was prevailed upon to go

to a revival meeting conducted by Sam Jones, the Billy Sunday of his time. Sam Jones had a style of preaching that was unique. He delivered his sermons just as though he were directing them to someone in the audience in particular. "Sister, you come to church with your best bonnet on and you didn't give your husband any breakfast this morning," or, "You old skinflint, you sit up here in church and you sing louder and pray longer than anyone, and your next door neighbor hasn't any milk for his little children and you have thirty cows and you wouldn't loan him one. You can't get to Heaven that way!" Of course, these seemingly personal examples of sin were his stock in trade—he used them in *every* town, knowing that his references were just general enough to fit someone present.

This particular revival was being held at Palisades Park at High Bridge, Kentucky. Here where the Dix River flows into the Kentucky, deep cliffs have been dug out by the water, and 315 feet above, the river is spanned by a railroad bridge. Palisades Park was then owned by the Southern Railroad and Sunday excursions from Cincinnati via Lexington were run across that bridge. The park comprised some seventy-five acres, commanding a sweeping view of the rivers; it boasted the usual soft drink stands, a bandstand where concerts were held, an open-sided auditorium, and a point jutting out over the river where your voice would echo and re-echo back to you. There were steps leading down the 315 feet of sheer cliff to the river, and it was here that Sam Jones was holding his revival. People from the neighboring counties flocked to hear him.

Uncle Will's presence at this revival was completely Sarah Eliza's doing. He had never heard Sam Jones preach. Aunt Sally planned to meet some of her Jessamine County relatives, have a box lunch together under the trees before the evening meeting, hear Sam Jones, and then drive the ten or twelve miles back home after the meeting was over. Sam preached twice a day and attended one of the basket suppers between the afternoon and evening sessions.

Just when the sermon was about to begin, both families—the Goddards and the Glaves—went into the auditorium to get seats. The place was rather crowded and Uncle Will decided to stand up in the back near the door. He removed his white felt hat and used it as a fan, occasionally stopping to brush a sleeve across his bald head. After the various announcements, scripture reading, prayers, and offerings, the sermon began.

Sam launched forth on his tirade. "There are a lot of people here who have no religion, standing around through curiosity. You old baldheaded devil, you leave your wife at home and go to chicken fights and bet on horses! Why don't you stay home with your wife and children? Bring your children up in the fear of God!"

All through the sermon Uncle Will fidgeted. Sam Jones was blasting out at swearing, chicken fighting, gambling on the horses, and not going to church. When the sermon finally ended, the preacher was in a sweat and the listeners were in a grand ecstasy of religious fervor. There were a number of converts. Uncle Will continued to fan.

The congregation filed out. And it seemed to Uncle Will that Sarah Eliza was certainly taking her time about getting out of the auditorium. She had to speak to everyone, and everyone there had to speak to her and pat the children on the head and exclaim over the wonderful sermon. He thought that she'd *never* come.

While he was fanning his more than ordinarily flushed face, one of his neighbors asked him what he thought of the sermon. "Oh, I reckon it was all right," Uncle Will replied, "but I must say that fellow got pretty damn personal!"

4

UNCLE WILL, SARAH ELIZA, AND THEIR CHILDREN

Uncle Will was born in 1819, the son of John Michael Goddard and Margaret McClary Goddard, whose father, a Methodist preacher, had been chaplain of Congress. A brother-in-law who was always called "Uncle Leuba" had been a rather famous musician and was said to have been music tutor to Louis Phillipe. When Louis Phillipe came to Nelson County, Kentucky, Uncle Leuba came with him and continued to live in the state.

Uncle Will's mother and father died when he was still a little boy, so Uncle Will came to live with the Berrys—his sister Evalina, her husband, and children. Though he was actually only a few years older, all of the nieces and nephews respectfully called him "Uncle Will." His favorite among them was John Berry—who was my grandfather.

Uncle Will and Grandfather looked so much alike that they were often mistaken for each other. In fact, one day when Uncle Will was about seventy years old, he was walking down the aisle of a Cincinnati store in the new suit and hat he'd just purchased when he suddenly saw John Berry approaching him. "By god, I'm damned glad to see you," he cried, and rushed up to clasp my grandfather's hand. He walked straight into the mirror at the front of the haberdashery.

Evalina's husband, George Berry, had been a colonel in the Union Army, and he was the only damyankee Uncle Will ever had a good word for. All through his life Uncle Will hated the damyankees with an intensity that cannot be comprehended now. He wouldn't allow any of his boys to wear blue suits because it had been the color of the Yankees' uniforms. Not until the boys were grown and had left home did they ever have blue clothes.

In fact, probably nowhere in the United States were feelings so divided over the Civil War and slavery as they were in Kentucky. Traditionally southern, Kentucky was nevertheless a border state and influenced by the North. Families were quite literally torn asunder by the war; father fought against son and brother against brother. So it was that George Berry's son Robert became a captain in the Confederate Army. On the eve of the battle of Cynthiana, Robert secured a leave of absence from General John Hunt Morgan and went to Lexington because he did not want to fight against his father. In that battle Colonel Berry was killed.

Perhaps I should say right out that Colonel Berry actually merited his rank in the Union Army. There's a story in Central Kentucky about an old Negro servant who persisted in calling every guest the family entertained either Doc or Colonel—including the visiting Admiral. Finally, the Admiral asked him how it was that so many colonels happened to live in Kentucky.

"There are three ways you gets to be a colonel in Kentucky," the old Negro told him. "A gentleman can fight in the war and get to be a colonel; the man in Frankfort can make you a colonel; and just lots of people gets to be a colonel by giving a poor old Negro like me a dollar."

My grandfather had a smart wife born a damyankee in Pennsylvania, but Uncle Will figured she couldn't help that. You see, Louisa Berry was just as unreconstructed a Rebel as he was. Although she had lost two brothers on the Union side and her father had been a Republican candidate for Congress, she took the Confederacy to her heart and hated Lincoln, Sherman, and Burbridge just as much as anybody. She was related to Julia Dent, wife of General Grant, but you'd never get her to admit it.

All during the Civil War Uncle Will was the most rampaging Rebel you could imagine. He didn't join the Confederate Army because of his wife and two children, but that didn't stop him from carrying on a guerrilla warfare of his own. In those days Black Joe usually pulled a buckboard full of rocks, which Uncle Will would throw with unerring aim whenever he spotted a Union sympathizer. Supplies were mysteriously set afire; horses got somehow unhitched from wagons, ran away, and were lost; Confederate soldiers were fed; information was given to the Confederate Army; and Uncle Will was damn proud of it!

One morning, as he was walking up the main street of Harrodsburg, a squad of Union soldiers stopped him and told him he was under arrest for aiding and abetting the enemy. As he was being led off, an onlooker asked Uncle Will where he was going. The inquirer knew well; his courage in asking probably derived from the eight soldiers who were guarding Mr. Goddard. "By god," exploded Uncle Will, "I'm going to Hell! Don't you see all these Devils around me?"

Actually, he was taken to Camp Chase and incarcerated for almost a year. And a few weeks after his imprisonment a son was born to Sarah Eliza. Before his enforced absence Mr. Goddard had declared that if the new baby were a boy he'd like him to be named for Stonewall Jackson; but now, Sarah Eliza wrote to her husband, asking about the child's name. The reply was, "I want the boy to be named for the whole glorious Confederacy. His name shall be Rebel Goddard." And so he was christened.

About this same time, a neighbor not far away who was a Union sympathizer named his son Union. This man became a great friend of Rebel Goddard in later years and the families intermarried.

Uncle Will was an impulsive, quick-tempered man who could hit hard and fast, and often did. He was never one to dodge an issue on any question whatsoever. He was a fighter, Uncle Will, and brave as a lion. On the other hand, he loved his family and his friends with an overwhelming affection. And he was just as proud of Sarah Eliza's family as he was of his own.

Soon after Uncle Will and Sarah Eliza were married, her brother Ed Glave and his wife Lizzie came to make a short visit; their visits lasted respectively for forty-five and forty-three years. So seductive were the charms of Wildwood that Brother Ed and Sister Lizzie simply extended the visit from month to month until in due course they were buried from Wildwood.

An insinuation that Uncle Will may or may not have intended has been read into a letter that he wrote to Sister Lizzie. At any rate, if he meant it, this letter holds the only hint he ever gave of being even a little vexed about the expense Mr. and Mrs. Glave had been to him. Their visit had already been prolonged over a period of several years when Uncle Will had occasion to write to Sister Lizzie from New Orleans. "My dear sister-in-law," the letter began, "and when I say dear, I mean dear for you have been dear to me."

But possible implications aside, the truth is that if Sarah Eliza had wanted a *dozen* brothers and sisters to live with them at Wildwood, Uncle Will would have tried to support and be kind to them and make the children obey them. In fact, any amount of company was all right with Uncle Will—just so they didn't get in his way and upset his plans.

On one occasion, Mamie, his eldest daughter, was giving a house party at Wildwood. Carrie Spillman, Jes-

samine and Kate Hemphill, Bird Martin, and Lizzie Berry had been there for a week. The girls enjoyed visiting at Wildwood because Glave and Nick and Reb could always be counted on to squire them around, and Mercer County had many other eligible young men who were eager to give the visiting ladies a rush.

Reb, Uncle Will's third son, was quite susceptible to feminine charms; at this time he was head over heels in love with Bird Martin. It was wheat cutting time at Wildwood and wheat cutting in those days was not carried out on a forty-hour-a-week schedule. Every minute that Reb could steal away from the field he spent talking with Bird on the front porch.

Twice already he had heard the hoofbeats of Black Joe just in time to sneak around the house before his father got there. This time Uncle Will galloped directly up to the porch. "Where in hell is that good-for-nothing Reb?" he shouted. "He's not in the wheat field and he's not here on the porch where I thought I'd find him." Looking both innocent and very beguiling in her white ruffled dress, Bird answered, "He must be in the wheat field, Mr. Goddard. He told me this morning at breakfast that he'd be cutting wheat all day. In fact, he asked me to come out and ride the binder, but it's too hot."

"A binder's not a buggy!" snorted Uncle Will, and galloped off to find Reb.

The Moores were giving a dance that night and Reb, of course, was going to take Bird. He had saved his money and bought a new Morrell Buggy without a top—"the better the moon to see." The colt that Uncle Will had given him was now three years old and it could trot a mile in close to three minutes. But he wouldn't be letting him out *tonight*, he thought.

As the day wore on, Reb was in more and more of a dither. Would they *never* finish cutting that field? The binder broke down, and Uncle Will had to go to Harrodsburg for a new piece for it; the wagon wheels got locked and had to be oiled and mended; *everything* went wrong. What had seemed like a job to be finished around 4 o'clock ran on to 6:00, then 6:30.

Finally the wheat was all in shocks, and Uncle Will went back to the house, leaving Reb to put up the binder and other farm machines and equipment. Uncle Will's inflexible rule was that every farming implement must be put under shelter immediately after using it and not be left out in the field overnight.

In his life Reb could not remember ever being in so much of a hurry. Putting up the binder would take nearly half an hour longer. For this once he decided to leave it where it was, and put it away the next morning before Papa got up.

At supper that night, for all Bird's blandishments, Reb was distrait. He was so afraid that Uncle Will would ask him if he had put up the binder that he could hardly eat any of the delicious food spread before him. Uncle Will would never sit down to a supper that had not at least two kinds of meat, cornbread and white flour biscuits or rolls, and all other suitable accompaniments. Tonight the meal consisted of fried game chicken and roast spring lamb from Uncle Will's flock of prizewinning Southdowns, cream gravy for the chickens and mint sauce for the lamb, beaten biscuits and corn pones, candied sweet potatoes, green beans, peas, corn pudding, okra, stewed onions, celery, sliced tomatoes as big as cantaloupes, and cottage cheese, watermelon sweet pickle, strawberry preserves, grape jelly, and blackberry cobbler with cream.

But now supper was over and Papa had still not mentioned the binder. As Reb left the table, his father said: "Early in the morning, Son, I want you to hitch up the team to the mower and cut those weeds in the Avenue. They are the goddamnedest growing weeds I ever saw!"

So Reb and Bird went off gaily to the dance, the arduous day entirely forgotten. It was 4:00 in the morning before the musicians played "Home Sweet Home" and the dancers kept begging for one more round. When the young people finally left the Moores, day was beginning to break. Reb was in no hurry to get home either; his fleet-footed colt ambled along at a slow walk.

All night the binder hadn't even entered Reb's mind. Now, as he turned in to Wildwood between the stone gateposts, he saw it on the other side of the fence. "Come with me, Bird," he cried, "I've got to hurry to the barn, get the team, and put the binder away before Papa starts out on his ride over the farm!"

He drove his colt to the barn as quickly as he could, geared up the team, brought the horses back to the binder, and hitched them to it. And there they were, coming up the Avenue, Reb on the lead horse, Bird seated on the binder, squealing "It's fun, isn't it?" when Uncle Will appeared out of nowhere, moving like a streak of lightning, straight toward them. He covered the distance between them in a couple of gallops, reigned in Black Joe, and held up his hand in front of the team. Then, with a "Whoa boys" to the horses, he caught hold of the bridle. Apparently, he never even noticed Bird's party dress nor Reb's Sunday suit, for he looked at Reb with pity. "Son," he said, "I told you to hitch up the team to the *mower* this morning to cut the weeds in the Avenue. And you've got the *binder!* You can't cut weeds with a binder! You're crazy as hell, by god! But I can't blame you," he added, looking at Bird. "She'd drive any man crazy!"

"Go on to the house now and eat your breakfast," he told them, "I'll get the mower and start cutting the weeds for you."

A phaeton full of people went from Wildwood to evening services each Sunday at the church in Harrodsburg. The Goddard boys went courting or stayed at home to entertain their sisters' guests. The Goddard girls had engagements with their special beaux. But these swains were under the watchful eye of Uncle Will.

If a young man appeared whom he didn't know, Uncle Will, much to the chagrin of the girls, would immediately open fire on him. "Where are you from? Who was your father?" and he'd look the young man over critically from head to foot.

At breakfast the next morning, likely as not, he'd say, "Mamie, that young man last night—by the name of Johnson—said he was from Pulaski County. I knew some mighty fast, bad actors named Johnson down around Somerset. They were drunkards and libertines. This young man might be one of their sons and, by god, I won't have one of my daughters marry into that family."

Mamie would try to convince her father that the young man was really a very decent sort, that he might have been of another family of Johnsons, and—more to the point—that she had no intention of marrying him anyhow. But Uncle Will took the chaperonage of his daughters seriously.

"It's all right to ask people to parties if they behave themselves, but it's a different matter when it comes to having an ornery, no-account fellow court my daughter."

Of course, among his own sons, it was Reb who was forever courting. If Reb couldn't find a buggy to drive, he'd sooner walk than miss out on a date. But Reb usually had a jumper, road horse, or saddle horse at his disposal, and being a good horseman he could handle all of them well.

Reb's courting ways didn't always set too well with Uncle Will, especially when there was a lot of work to do on the farm. On one particular day, late in the afternoon, Reb was riding down the Avenue on a young jumper he'd trained when Uncle Will spied him. Reb knew that there was a good deal of work ahead; if he turned back now, he'd never see his girl that night. So he kept right on going—and Uncle Will followed, urging Black Joe along, calling and cursing all the while. Black Joe was a fast little pony, and Uncle Will gained on them right away, but just as he got close, Reb touched the colt with his heel and whoosh! they were over the rail fence!

Now, as far as Uncle Will was concerned, Black Joe had only two faults: he couldn't talk, and he wouldn't jump. As for the ability to talk, it hardly mattered, since Uncle Will would never have given that horse an opportunity to say anything anyway. By god, he, W. W. Goddard, would do all the talking! But Black Joe refused to jump, Uncle Will couldn't make him, and he had to yield—he who yielded to the whims of neither man nor beast. (Of course he gave in to Sarah Eliza's wishes now and again; but she was the best wife any man ever had.)

When Reb's colt jumped the rail fence, Uncle Will had no choice but to ride down the Avenue to the road and open the gate into the field to catch up with them. And now when he got within shouting distance once again, that colt jumped right back over the rail fence, forcing Uncle Will to turn back, go through the gate on the turnpike and chase them up the Avenue. And of course when Uncle Will caught up again, Reb's horse jumped right back into the field.

Uncle Will was fit to be tied. As he continued up the Avenue to the house, he hollered over to Reb, "Go on, by god, bread and meat will bring you home!"

Reb wasn't the only Goddard boy who came under fire. Ralph and Paul were forever getting foolish looking clothes! A regular pair of dudes, Uncle Will called them. Looking askance at Paul's new black "tooth-pick" shoes, he'd exclaim, "By god, I have to walk around them like rockers on a chair!" As Uncle Will saw it, neatness was all that was necessary.

One day Ralph asked Uncle Will to let him have $2.00.

"For what?" he said. "You get paid Saturday night, and this is only Monday."

"Well," said Ralph, "I want to buy a pocketbook to keep my money in."

"For god's sake, what do you want with a pocketbook if you haven't got anything to put in it?"

Uncle Will thought that his daughters were bright, attractive girls, but "not half so good-looking and smart as their mother." Except in the matter of chaperonage he left their upbringing to Sarah Eliza, but he did have his say about their foibles.

When Rea was about eighteen years old the fashion for young ladies was shirtwaists and skirts with black taffeta collars and belts. One day when my mother asked him a perfectly innocent question about how Rea was feeling lately, Uncle Will saw his chance: "How can she be well?" he exploded, "She winds yards and yards of black ribbon around her waist so tight she can't breathe. And then she winds yards and yards of the same stuff around her neck until her eyes pop out! You can't do anything with her because she's hell for style!"

Uncle Will was a great believer in system. He was up before anyone on the place and the last in bed; every morning before breakfast he rode over all of Wildwood planning the work for the day. He was a good manager and knew how to keep the boys and men busy. Even on rainy days there were a thousand things to do.

In his personal affairs Uncle Will was a constant willmaker; as his finances mounted or dropped Uncle Will made changes in his bequests. When tobacco was high and Uncle Will had sold some colts by Sumpter Denmark for a big price he would write another will and up the bequests he was to give this friend or that relative. "One damn thing is sure, by god, when I die, Sarah Eliza will have no financial worries." And she didn't, although she outlived her husband by many years.

Uncle Will made all his plans for his funeral before he died. In fact, years before his death he went shopping for his coffin in Cincinnati. When he found just the kind he wanted, he bought it, had it sent to Wildwood, and put it under his bed. There it stayed until his death.

Incidentally, on this particular trip to Cincinnati Uncle Will was also attracted by an auctioneer who was about to sell a split second watch. Uncle Will had been needing a watch like that, by god; those timers never timed the horses right in the races at Lexington. As was the custom, the watch was passed around; Uncle Will examined it—and kept it, holding it up for all to see. Then when he'd made the last bid, he simply dropped the watch into the pocket of his linen duster, walked up to the auctioneer, handed him the money he had bid, and prepared to leave. The bookkeeper was visibly disturbed; he insisted upon wrapping the watch before Uncle Will took it home. No indeed, said Uncle Will, he would not give up the watch. Again the bookkeeper in-

sisted, the manager came up, the auctioneer stopped the sale—it was a rule of the auction that all articles must be wrapped. "No, by god, I bought this watch and I'm going to keep it so that I'll know it's the same watch I bought!" And keep it he did.

Later he was told that the auction was closed by the police for selling fraudulent goods: the bookkeeper was substituting cheaper articles for the ones the buyers gave him to wrap.

Uncle Will was always happy about company, and parties were fine with him; only he wanted a lot of people invited, no neighbors slighted, and plenty of good solid food that would stick to your ribs. He wouldn't tolerate pretense or sham or put-on in his house. His idea of entertaining was a good informal time with a lot of good people. He hated these stiff, formal parties where nobody had a good time and nothing was fit to eat.

Ina, his second daughter, had her own ideas about the kind of party to have at Wildwood; she was about twenty-one at the time, and wanted to give a party that would be even more meticulously planned than the beautiful reception Mrs. Dan Moore had recently given at Mooreland. Since Uncle Will had gone to New Orleans on business, this seemed to be the perfect time. With Papa out of the house, she could invite the people from Harrodsburg, Danville, Lawrenceburg, and Lexington to whom she was obligated, serve the kind of food in vogue at that time, and have the whole party over the day before he came home. She began to make her preparations.

She had engraved invitations sent out to about one hundred ladies. She ordered individual ices in pink flower designs, little individual pink iced cakes, pink mints, and nuts from Benedict's in Louisville. And she bought a new, long-trained, red satin dress trimmed in jet and black lace in Cincinnati.

The afternoon before the reception her friends came

44

by to assist, bringing baskets of garden flowers, some even bringing roses and carnations from the florist. They helped her decorate the whole house with baskets and vases of flowers: yellow flowers in the hall, red flowers in the parlors, pink flowers in the dining room. On the dining room table she set pink candles and a silver basket with pink roses. Later, silver bowls with the pink mints, and silver cake baskets with the pink cakes would be placed there.

She asked Ned and Willy to take all the leaves out of the table for what was probably the first time since it had been enlarged to serve the first guests who came to Wildwood after Uncle Will and Aunt Sally had married and moved into the big house. She then had it covered with the hand drawn lace cloth she had worked on for several years and been saving for the occasion. The family would just have to eat in the pantry or kitchen or off the sideboard until after the reception.

Smilax had been twined around the pillars in the back hall and around the stair rail, and Willy and Ned and Silas moved the furniture to make more room for the guests. Ina thought that the house had never looked so beautiful!

She was up early on the day of the party to put fresh water in the vases so that none of the flowers would die, and to see that the finishing touches were given to everything. She was feeling excited and happy about the party—she just knew that everything was going to be lovely!

Suddenly she was conscious of the whirlwind that invariably accompanied Uncle Will, and she hadn't even time to gather her thoughts together when he was there in front of her. He had finished his business in New Orleans earlier than expected and decided to come on home. He had gotten off the train at Burgin and been driven to Wildwood by Nim Buster. "A goddamn slow horse he was driving, too. I told him he ought to have a horse like Black Joe."

Immediately Uncle Will sensed the activities in the air. Ina was having a party. Well that was fine, of course, but had she invited Mrs. Long at the tollgate? "Did you invite Mrs. Welch?" he asked. "Surely you asked all the Gaithers and the Moores and the Colemans? What do you mean just one out of a family? They're our neighbors and you didn't ask *all* of them? Well! by god, I'll send Ned on horseback to invite the others!" Uncle Will thereupon called the yardman and told him to go to all the houses in the neighborhood and ask the ladies if they had received their invitations to Miss Ina's party. If they had not, they were invited anyway and were to come at 4 o'clock that afternoon.

"What are you going to have for your company to eat, Ina?" Uncle Will asked, rushing back into the house.

He looked at the individual ices and cakes.

"Is that *all?*" he exploded. "Well, by god, I'll not have people driving to Wildwood three, five, ten, fifteen miles, and more, to give them a little dab of ice cream and a thimbleful of cake! All of you ought to be glad I got home when I did. Asking people to come all those miles and then starving them to death! It's not hospitable! It's not right! By god, I'll barbecue two lambs and cut some two-year-old hams. Tell Kizzie to make light rolls and beaten biscuits. Send Willy and Silas here to me. We'll build a platform under a big tree."

Uncle Will rushed here and there giving orders and directing activities. By 3 o'clock the platform and food were ready for the company to arrive. There was more than enough for Ina's invited guests and the hundred others that he had invited combined. He went through the window to change to a clean linen suit, put on another black string bow tie, and shine his congress gaiters.

By god, he'd done a good job and helped Ina out of a hole. It would have been a goddamn shame to have people come that far in the country and give them such little food as Ina had for them. Now—to go out and min-

46

gle with the company. Perhaps some of the Cynthiana kin would be there.

He dashed back out the window onto the porch and came around to the front of the house. At the front door he saw Willy standing in a white coat holding a silver tray in his hand.

"What are you doing here, Willy?" he shouted. "Get back to the kitchen where you belong!"

"But Marse Will," said Willy, "Miss Ina done tole me to stan' at de door and meets de guests."

"Get out of here, you black devil you, and tell Miss Ina to come here this minute."

Ina came running to Uncle Will.

"What are you thinking of Ina? All this highfalutin' nonsense. *I'll* receive the guests at Wildwood *myself!*"

And he did, too; as the ladies drove up in their carriages and buggies he met them and helped them out. After ordering Silas and Ned to tie the horses in the shade and undo the overchecks so that the horses would be comfortable, he gallantly escorted the ladies to the platform under the elm tree where large slices of ham and barbecued lamb, light rolls, pears, and watermelon were served to them before they went into the house.

Never one to apologize, Uncle Will did, however, express regret that he had not known about the party in time to have a repast worthy of the company.

Uncle Will seldom failed to get in the last word and rarely was he unable to succeed in having his own way. There were occasions, however . . . .

One morning he was riding over the Van Arsdell place, a piece of ground on the extreme back boundary of Wildwood. Fields in Kentucky were not called the North 40, the East 60, etc. as they were in the West; each field had its own particular name. One field was called the Ashe thicket, another the Woods' acres, another the Dripping Spring field; and one field that was rather remote and the only untillable land at Wildwood was known as Egypt. The Van Arsdell place was a field of fifty acres or so that at one time had belonged to the Van Arsdell family.

On this particular morning as Uncle Will rode along the fence row next to the Bohon pike, he saw some gypsies camped just inside the gate in the Van Arsdell place. A redhaired woman was cooking breakfast over a fire made with firewood that had just recently been rails in Uncle Will's fence; a man stood near the fence, holding an axe.

Uncle Will rode up to the man and in his sternest voice said, "Do you know whose land this is?" The gypsy shook his head. Only then did the redheaded cook look up.

"Why don't you bring the kindling?" she said. "The fire's low. What does the man on the black horse say?"

"He asks," said the gypsy, "if I know whose land this is." In the meantime Uncle Will had taken off his hat and was mopping his brow.

"Well, you tell him it's God Almighty's land. Bring me that kindling and don't waste your time talking to that interfering old baldheaded fool."

It is said that Uncle Will turned without a word and rode away. He had met defeat for the second time. Once by a black stud pony who refused to jump, and now by a redheaded gypsy woman who told him off. These are the only setbacks I know of where he neither got in the last word nor had the last blow.

Perhaps as he rode home, a little chastened, he pondered for awhile on what had just happened. More likely he didn't. After all, there was so much to do and so little time to do it! By god, he was in a hell of a hurry and he must get those lazy trifling hands to work!

5

THEY'RE TOO DAMN
GOOD TO SELL

Uncle Will was a good farmer, and Wildwood was a good farm. The soil was deep with an underlying stratum of limestone, and Uncle Will saw to it that red clover and bluegrass seed were sowed regularly, and that his pastures were mowed twice a year. He knew that if bluegrass were given the chance, it would eventually crowd out the weeds. Moreover, tobacco grew best on bluegrass sod plowed and turned over. Burley was grown at Wildwood, but because it took so much from the soil, it was never raised more than two years in the same field. Corn, hay, oats, wheat, and hemp were also raised in abundance. In the fall, after the tobacco or corn or hemp was cut, Uncle Will always sowed a cover crop to keep the soil from washing.

"By god," he'd proclaim, "Wildwood is the best farm in the whole South!"—and when Uncle Will said South he meant the world. His pride in the farm was by no means unjustified either: he paid a great deal of attention to it. He had the best possible ponds and cisterns and wells to furnish water for his stock. "Did you ever see such a fine, cold spring," he'd declare rather than ask, "as that one under the springhouse?"

He was an able husbandman too. He knew how to put

flesh on livestock, horses, cattle, hogs, and sheep. Of necessity he was a financier, an economist, and something of a mechanic. He not only directed and managed, but was often obliged to instruct his hands in the methods of farming procedure.

Like all good Central Kentucky farms, throughout Uncle Will's life, Wildwood was practically self-sustaining. During the first decade of his tenure everything that was used on the farm, with the exceptions of coffee, tea, sugar, salt, spices, nails, horseshoes, farm implements, and an occasional silk dress for Sarah Eliza, was produced at Wildwood.

Before the War between the States, when a house was constructed in Central Kentucky, all materials used were from the farm. The wood for beams, floors, window and door frames and trims, stairways, wainscoting, baseboards, and chair rails all came from walnut or oak or ash trees on the estate. The trims and mantels were often carved by itinerant cabinetmakers and woodcarvers. Slaves were apprenticed to the nearest brick plants to learn the composition of bricks. A kiln was set up in the yard, and bricks for the new house were manufactured on the place. Glass for the windows, lamps, and chandeliers, and wall paper and paint, of course, all had to be ordered from the city. But the hardware was sometimes fashioned on the place by the slave who served as the farm blacksmith with the help of an assistant.

The vegetables, fruits, and meats for the table were all raised at Wildwood. Some fruits and vegetables were canned for use during winter; sweet potatoes were buried to be dug up as needed; irish potatoes, turnips, onions, and apples were stored in the cellar. Chickens were raised for the young friers and broilers, for hens in the wintertime, and for eggs at all times. Unlike some estates, Wildwood boasted no mill, so corn and wheat had to be sent either to the Shaker grist mill or to another mill nearby. Here the grain was ground into meal and flour, and the miller took a percentage of it in payment for the grinding.

Uncle Will loved to tell about the minister who sent a young slave to Paul's Mill, not far from Wildwood, one Sunday morning to get some flour. The slave was to negotiate with the miller and then appear at church in the balcony with the other slaves. When the boy finally got to the church, his master was already in the pulpit, preaching on Saul's conversion along the Damascus Road. "And what did Paul say?" he exhorted—whereupon the black boy rose up and answered, "Paul say, you can't have no more flour till you send him some wheat for the last you gits."

Fall was hog killing time at Wildwood, and the occasion amounted almost to a festival. The ladies helped to season the sausage and then "tried" it by cooking small cakes on the stove. The children made balloons of dried hog bladders and popped them over one another's heads. The succulent hog meat (never spoken of as pork) was trimmed and dressed. Fresh sausage, tenderloins, and spareribs were sent to relatives. Feasts of the tender morsels were spread before the family. Side meat for bacon, shoulders, and jowls were salted down and smoked to last throughout the year. The hams were cured and smoked to hang for two years before they were served with pride by Uncle Will. Sausage was stuffed in bags to keep through the winter. Lard was rendered from the fatty scraps. The Negroes had their fill of pigs feet, hogs heads, pigs tails, and chitterlings.

Another festive occasion of the fall was the grinding of the sorghum cane, the boiling of the syrup, and the "stir off." The sorghum molasses was poured into gallon buckets to be used as "long sweetening" in gingerbread, black fruit cake, molasses candy, and as a syrup on soda biscuits, corn battercakes, and wheat cakes. Cider making too added zest to the autumn days.

The oversupply of eggs, butter, cottage cheese, and

fresh vegetables in the summer, and of sorghum, cider, and possibly hog meat in the fall were taken to the store in Harrodsburg and used as credit throughout the year for coffee, sugar, salt, spices, an occasional length of dress goods, or a kitchen utensil.

Lambs and beeves were slaughtered when needed for the table. Wool was carded for dresses and suits. The hides from the slaughtered beeves were taken to the local cobbler to be tanned and made into shoes.

Wheat, hemp, and tobacco were sold. The hay, oats, and corn were raised to feed the livestock. "He's a god-damn poor farmer, no-account and trifling," Uncle Will would exclaim of any man who bought feed for his stock. "If I couldn't raise my own feed, by god, I'd know I was in the wrong business. When I bought those two hundred steers cheap, I did have to buy a little corn to feed them out, but that was different. I'd never have to buy feed for my regular stock."

All the mules on the farm were bred there, and the best heifer calves were kept for milch cows. Lambs, hogs, calves, mules, and a good colt now and then were sold off the farm, and these, along with the wheat, hemp, and tobacco served as the money crops.

The tobacco grown at Wildwood was heavier in texture than present day Burley. Uncle Will had exhibited a stalk of it in Chicago in the '80s and won a music box for the best tobacco in the show. Uncle Will loved to show people this music box and he played it with great pride. Its tinkling strains of "The Blue Danube" and "Listen to the Mocking Bird" are inextricably woven into the atmosphere of Wildwood.

That prize-winning tobacco brought 10¢ a pound! So phenomenal was this price at the time that Uncle Will declared: "If I knew that I could get 10¢ a pound for all the tobacco I raised, by god, I'd plow up the whole 325 acres of Wildwood and put every damn one in tobacco." How surprised he'd be today by the finely textured cigarette tobacco developed from the same type of Burley he raised; in 1918 it went for $1.25 a pound!

The wheat and hemp crops required labor on the part of every able-bodied man on the farm—Uncle Will, all the Goddard boys, the Negroes, harvest hands, and hemp breakers. At threshing and hemp breaking times, life at Wildwood was pretty hectic with all the harvest hands to be fed and Uncle Will's stirring the boys out at daybreak to keep them at work until sunset.

There were always a lot of Negroes at Wildwood, even after the war. Most of them had gone at first, just after the Emancipation Proclamation; only Silas had asked if he and Kizzie and their family could stay on in their cabin and continue to work for "Marse Will" and "Miz Sarah Liza." But then, during the next year or two, three or four more families came back, and they stayed on at Wildwood too.

As a horse breeder and developer, Uncle Will was without peer. He had bought Sumpter Denmark as a yearling for $500, which at that time (1865) was the highest price ever paid for a saddle colt. Even Sarah Eliza must have been greatly disturbed by this seeming extravagance. About eight years later Sumpter Denmark won his cost price in St. Louis—at that time the highest stake ever offered in a saddle horse ring; he was first in a ring of nineteen, among them such famous horses as Peavine 85, Montrose, and the Adkin's mare. In that same year he won the largest stake that had ever been given in Kentucky.

As a show horse, Sumpter Denmark won premiums totalling many times the amount paid for him; as a sire, he became one of the foundations of the American saddle horse. He was a good harness horse too, and Uncle Will often drove him to the buckboard, particularly when he had business at George Handy's. Although the trip was eight miles by road and involved a number of gates along the way, it was less than half that much across the fields. That trip across the fields would have made a good obstacle race to test the ability of any horse, but Sumpter Denmark had been taught to jump fences and creeks, to climb up steep grades, and to descend deep cliffs. He was a fine horse!

Even in those days, there were people who derided the stamina of the thoroughbred. They said that the race had degenerated, that style and speed and more speed had taken their toll. The high bred horses were not as tough as they used to be. I suppose that ever since the days of Bellerophon the same thing has been said. "You remember that imported Meddler? There was a horse. No horse could stand up against him today."

Well, I have in mind a particular day, when Uncle Will had decided to drive Sumpter to George Handy's by way of the turnpike. He had just about completed his business there when Pete came running up the avenue, out of breath and covered with dust. "Marse Will," he gasped, "Miz Sarah Eliza sent me to fetch you. Mr. Glave hit Mr. Reb over the eye with the axe. You better come quick!" Glave had been chopping wood, he said, and the head of the axe slipped off.

Uncle Will immediately began to unhitch Sumpter Denmark from the buckboard. Calling to George Handy to lend him a saddle and bridle, and hollering at Pete to undo the checkrein before he did the traces and to unwrap the shaft bands first, he was in a turmoil. He seemed to have three or four voices at once and even more bodies, whereas an even dozen linen dusters were all over the place. Mr. Handy hadn't even a chance to ask why he wanted a saddle or what he was going to ride. No time for explanations, only orders and directions!

Uncle Will was already swinging into the saddle. As he kicked Sumpter in the side with his right heel, he reached down, picked up Pete, and put him up behind

him on the saddle. To Sumpter that heel-kick, firm but not violent, and Uncle Will's leaning forward to grab up Pete meant a canter off on the right foot, about like a rocking chair, with the rhythm of 1, 2, 3, 4. That canter lasted only a short time. At his master's urging Sumpter swung into a long low gallop. Over the rail fence and down the steep incline to the creek at the bottom they went, a sure-footed gallant horse, a confident horseman riding with the breeding of generations and the experience of fifty years, and Pete, holding on for dear life. Down hill and up hill they rode, over fences, across creeks, with never a falter by Sumpter and ever encouragement from Uncle Will. The only noises to be heard were quickly falling hoofs, "easy boy" and "atta boy," all merging into a long and steady rhythmic pattern.

"Pete," said Uncle Will, "we left Mr. Handy's house at 3:46 and we'll be at Wildwood before 4 o'clock! That's something no other horse in the world can do!"

Reb was not hurt badly. A little fat meat on his eye and a stitch or two by Dr. Robards were all that he needed.

But the ride was remarkable. The next issue of the *Harrodsburg Herald* carried an ad that read: "I, W. W. Goddard, will give any man $1,000 who can ride cross country from George Handy's corn crib to the stiles at Wildwood in 13 minutes. Sumpter Denmark did it with me on his back and a Negro boy behind me." There were no takers.

His own proclivities notwithstanding, Uncle Will insisted on Sarah Eliza's driving a gentle horse. Sarah Eliza rather liked a spirited horse herself, and she was not averse to racing Mrs. Coleman on the turnpike on the way home from church services. However, Uncle Will had given standing orders: if she drove in the buggy with one or more of the girls, she must have a gentle horse; if Willy or Silas or Ned or one of her sons drove her in the phaeton or carriage, she must have a gentle horse. "You just can't trust one of those boys not to do some goddamn foolish thing and break all of your necks, and I won't have it," expostulated Uncle Will.

In any case, Sarah Eliza and the children always went to church in style. And afterwards, the dinner table, literally groaning with food, would always be surrounded by the members of the family and their company. At 2:30, all the ladies would go upstairs to take naps, and all the men went with Uncle Will to walk around the farm and look over the barns.

First of all they'd look at Sumpter Denmark and admire his many fine points and talk about his abilities in the show ring and in stud.

Then Uncle Will would expatiate on King of Sharon: "No better bull was ever bred than King of Sharon. Abe Renick sold his father for several thousand dollars, and his mother was a direct descendant of old Rose of Sharon herself. He's a 'Thirty-seven' and from the 'Bates' line too. By god, I'll have only 'Thirty-sevens' at Wildwood!" The "Thirty-sevens" were descendants of the first shorthorns imported by Lewis Sanders in 1837. (A few years later, of course, Henry Clay began to import shorthorns too.) Shorthorns, thought to be the long-sought dual purpose cattle—excellent both for milk and for beef—were the talk of the day. Fortunes were made and lost on these red, white, and roan cattle.

Next the men came to the Southdown sheep, fifteen or twenty yearling rams of which Uncle Will was going to sell. "They're really too damn good to sell. They'll all win at Chicago. I ought to keep them and show them."

Then, as Uncle Will led the group to the jack barn, he'd say, "What about that Jack Spann? Did you ever see such an ear and foot on a jack in your life? He measures fifteen hands and two inches."

In a pen nearby were the game chickens. Uncle Will once sold a dozen of those stags to a man in New York for what then seemed almost a fabulous price.

After looking at the tobacco growing in the fields or hanging in the tobacco barns, and going through the orchard, the men would come back to the house about 4 o'clock to join the ladies who looked pretty and refreshed after their naps. Neighbors and relatives and beaux dropped in. If it was summer all sat out in the yard. And then out came those wonderful watermelons! At other times of the year ruddy apples, ginger cake and cider, or ice cream and cake were passed around to all present.

Some of the company would stay to Sunday-night supper—just a cold snack of chicken, ham, cottage cheese, tomatoes, cucumbers, celery, beaten biscuits, buttered lightbread, blackberry jelly, strawberry jam, watermelon pickles, devilled eggs, potato salad, apple pie, ice cream, devil's food cake, white pound cake, with hot tea and coffee.

Many great saddle horses, trotters, and thoroughbreds were bred at Wildwood by Uncle Will. Furthermore, his Southdown sheep and shorthorn cattle testified to his ability as a judge and producer of livestock. Uncle Will was actually quite an enthusiastic admirer of shorthorns in general. He showed his own at fairs and expositions, traded them, sold several for large prices, and attended many shorthorn meetings and sales.

Once in the late '90s, the Shorthorn Breeders Association gave a banquet that was all but interminable. This was at the Phoenix Hotel in Lexington; livestock men from all over Kentucky and the South were present. Uncle Will had driven over from Harrodsburg with Reb, who was home from the West on a visit. After mint juleps (of which Uncle Will disapproved), the men sat down to oyster soup, roast turkey with dressing and sausage cakes, old baked ham, cranberry sauce, celery, pickles, candied yams, peas, butterbeans, mashed potatoes, chicken salad, tutti-frutti ice cream, pecan cake, angel food cake, and coffee. About 9 o'clock the speeches began. Eight short speeches were listed on the program, each to extol some phase of the glorious shorthorn, and each to last about five minutes.

As it turned out, the first speaker spoke thirty-five minutes—and closed with an apology, for he had in no way exhausted his subject. Only the toastmaster's eagle eye had kept him from going on. The next speaker spoke for forty-five minutes; and the remaining six were no different. It was nearly 1 o'clock, and the banquet was just getting warmed up. Now they were calling on extemporaneous speakers. Uncle Will, as one of the veteran shorthorn breeders of Kentucky, was acclaimed and asked to speak. And speak he did. He rose to his feet and said:

"I like shorthorn cattle and, by god, all of you know I do. I like to talk about them and to hear about them. But I can't stay here all night listening to speeches. I have been to many a banquet in my life, but this is the goddamnedest longest one I have ever attended! Long speeches about shorthorns; by god, that's funny! I reckon since nobody in Kentucky has any desire to leave the state and go to Heaven, God Almighty has punished us with hell on earth in the way of long banquets and goddamn tiresome banquet speeches. Goodnight, I like all of you, but I am on my way to Wildwood." And Uncle Will, followed by Reb, fled the banquet hall.

Since Uncle Will was one of the leading farmers of Mercer County, director of the American Shorthorn Breeders Association, director of the Mercer County Fair, and on the board of many farm organizations, he was naturally approached for his opinion in regard to innovations. When the idea of using the Osage orange hedge to fence in livestock became popular, a promoting firm of nurserymen in a neighboring state asked a representative from each section of Kentucky to come up to see the plantings. The Osage oranges were supposed to revolutionize fencing: they had only to be planted, allowed to grow, and then trimmed to the desired height. The hedge would make a practical, good-looking fence that would turn any stock. Uncle Will was invited from his district.

A large field had been set out with hedges in various sizes, some trimmed low to the ground, some four feet, some six feet, some even higher, and the presentation was a beautiful sight. Uncle Will inspected these hedges very thoroughly.

"What do you think of the hedges, Mr. Goddard?" one of the nurserymen asked him.

"Very pretty! Very pretty!" said Uncle Will.

"And what will you tell your neighbors back home when they ask you about the hedges, Mr. Goddard?"

"I'll tell them that they're very pretty."

"But will you tell them anything else, Mr. Goddard?"

"Yes; if they ask me, I'll tell them they'll have to nurse them by god for five years and fight them for fifty!"

By all the rules of horse trading, Uncle Will should never have been a good trader. He was too forthright, too expressive of his feelings, too lacking in suavity, too honest to be the proverbial horse trader. He hated a lie; a liar was nearly as bad as a damyankee. But Uncle Will had a knowledge of horses; he possessed the almost uncanny ability to look at a horse and *know* that it would or would not develop into a fast horse or a show horse. I have seen only a few people in my lifetime who had this gift. They recognize a certain look that the horse has, the way he carries himself.

Uncle Will owned many kinds of horses: the very best, like Sumpter Denmark, Fanny Witherspoon, Ella Breckinridge, and Red Leaf; plucky, dependable, non-pedigreed horses like Black Joe; and some like the roan gelding that Reb took to sell at W. H. Wilson's auction.

W. H. Wilson was a fine horse breeder; he had once owned George Wilkes, one of the greatest stallions of all time. A few years before, when he had found himself in straitened circumstances, he sold chances on his famous show horse Lady de Jarnette for ten dollars apiece. Hundreds were sold far and wide, for everybody hoped to own this grand mare. Later he bought her back from the lucky lottery winner.

Mr. Wilson had built a half-mile track a little way out of Cynthiana, and it was here, at Abdallah Park, that he held his sales. Uncle Will was sending a consignment of three or four horses to this one. Reb had left Wildwood four days beforehand to travel the sixty miles, riding one of the horses and leading the others.

The first night he stopped at my father's farm; the second he stayed with General Withers. Reb always enjoyed visiting the Withers family; among other reasons, there was a daughter in the family just about his age, who, incidentally, was also named Rebel. The third night he stayed with the Clays in Bourbon County, and arrived the next day in Cynthiana, where he and his horses were put up for the night at Jim Cromwell's.

W. H. Wilson's sale was scheduled for 9 o'clock Friday morning, and Uncle Will had planned to be there to represent his horses himself. However, when the time came to sell the Wildwood string, Uncle Will was nowhere in sight, so Reb proceeded to tell the buyers of the horses' respective virtues. The first one up for sale was the roan gelding. Reb had always particularly liked that horse; he had done a lot of courting with him hitched to his high wheeled, no-top buggy. He, therefore, waxed eloquent over him.

The bidding was brisk. It started at $150 and went to $175; then $200, $225, $250, $275, $300. Reb again spoke affectionately of the horse, said that although he was gentle he could trot a streak. A new bidder raised the bid to $325. Someone else bid $350. Just then Uncle Will flew in like a bat out of hell, his linen duster whipping behind him as he came.

"Stop!" he shouted, as he reached the auctioneer's stand. "How much are you bid on that roan horse?"

"Three hundred and fifty dollars, Mr. Goddard," answered the auctioneer.

"Hellfire," said Uncle Will, "sell him quick. That's $150 more than he's worth!"

It was Uncle Will's custom to stop the bidding on his horses when he thought that they were bringing their just prices. The buyer always knew that when Will Goddard said a horse was worth a certain amount, the horse was really worth that much. In the end, Uncle Will's honesty actually led to his being an excellent horse trader.

At another sale in Cynthiana, Uncle Will was selling a mare that Sarah Eliza had driven to the buggy. The mare was so afraid of trains that whenever one came by she stood still and quaked. But she had never tried to run away except when Uncle Will was driving her; he scared her even worse than the trains did. When Uncle Will heard the train coming, he'd whip up the mare to try to beat the train to the crossing. He finally decided to sell her, and it fell to Reb's lot to ride her through the country to another of W. H. Wilson's sales at Abdallah Park.

Once again, Reb was staying at Jim Cromwell's, and the night before the sale, Jim asked Reb about the mare that his mother had driven. He said that he wanted a nice horse for Belle (his wife), and that Belle hated a broken-down, spiritless horse.

Reb explained that the mare was a little skittish at trains but a great deal more afraid of Papa. "Mama's driven her everyplace," he said, "including church, and to prayer meeting on Wednesday nights. That mare can trot too. With Mama driving she can out-trot Mrs. Coleman's Cyclone filly every time." Reb said further that she was a well-bred mare with a long neck and that she could raise a fine colt or two by Harrison Chief. In fact, for a young man, Reb was such a good sales and horseman that Jim Cromwell decided to bid on the mare the next day.

Rebel Goddard and James Cromwell, the boy and the man, found much of mutual interest to discuss. They talked of horses and shorthorn cattle, and the new sensational trotter, Maud S. Some predicted that this wonder-mare would trot a mile in 2:10—but that was preposterous! *

By half past eight all were in bed because tomorrow would be a big day with lots of company. Jim Cromwell was a lot like Uncle Will; in fact, they were congenial on many points. Like Uncle Will, he was the soul of hospitality, and he'd probably bring home six or seven or eight friends with him from the sale. Belle knew how to prepare good food and he was proud of her dinners.

Uncle Will was coming down to the sale on the L & N train from Lexington. He was supposed to arrive about 8 o'clock, but this morning of all mornings the train was late. John Throckmorton, the conductor, tried to console Uncle Will, but Uncle Will would not be comforted.

"I'll never ride your damn train again!" he fumed. "I wanted to drive Black Joe but Sarah Eliza talked me out of it. Women are *always* getting you late to places!" But then, of course, Sarah Eliza was the best woman in the world. When Uncle Will thought of Sarah Eliza and the nine children and Wildwood he often forgot to be impatient because, by god, he was the most fortunate man on earth.

"But, dammit, John, your train could go a little faster! I'll miss that sale, and Reb may make a fool of himself and that mare. Why in hell do you wait so long in Paris? Asa Jewell wanted me to come down last night with him

* A little later, Maud S. lowered the world's record for a trotter to 2.08¾.

63

to Berry Station and stay at John's. We could have driven from there to Cynthiana in no time and been at Wilson's around half past seven." Uncle Will fretted and cussed. The time for the sale came and went, and he was still on the train.

The auction started promptly at 9 o'clock. The terms were read: All sales were for cash; animals were guaranteed as to "eyes, wind, and work"; and the owner and the seller were not responsible for the horse after the auctioneer knocked him down to the buyer.

The horses were sold on the track, with Mr. Wilson standing in front of the auctioneer's stand. As each horse was brought onto the track, the auctioneer would read his pedigree and Mr. Wilson would look into the horse's mouth to see how old he was and briefly scrutinize his legs.

The crowd in front of the stand divided into two lines as the horse was ridden, driven, or led up and down the track to show his gait and speed. After two or three times up and down, the horse was ordered to stop in front of the auctioneer's stand, and the owner would make a brief statement about the horse's speed, training, and general disposition. Then the auctioneer asked for bids; under $100 no increase of less than $5.00 would be accepted; over $100 the bids had to be of $10.00 or more.

That morning Sarah Eliza's buggy mare was the fourth horse up for sale. Reb was showing her to a break-cart that he had borrowed from Jim Cromwell, and he had rubbed her down until her coat shone like satin. He let her trot up and down the track several times to demonstrate her speed.

When the auctioneer blew his whistle for Reb to bring her to the stand, the crowd seemed interested in her. Reb told them that she had been his mother's mare, that his mother had driven her everyplace. She was a little afraid of steam cars, but she was a nice, usually well-mannered mare. She was by Red Wilkes and would make someone a mighty good buy.

Mr. Cromwell started her at $100. Someone raised the bid to $150. "Two hundred dollars," said Mr. Cromwell. "Two hundred twenty-five," said someone else. The bid was raised to $250, $275. Then Mr. Wilson stepped in and said that he'd make one bid of $300. Mr. Cromwell bid $325.

Just at that moment Uncle Will came rushing into the crowd, linen duster and all, swearing at the L & N Railroad, at John Throckmorton, and at the general cussedness of the world.

"What in hell did Reb tell you," he shouted, "to make you bid so much on that mare? Who's bidding on her anyway?"

The auctioneer said that Mr. Cromwell had just bid $325, and Jim Ward bid $350.

Uncle Will stood erect in all his five-feet-seven-inch dignity, took off his white felt hat, and said in a loud voice:

"Jim Cromwell, if you're buying this mare for Belle, I'm sorry to hear that you don't love her any more and want her out of the way. Buy the mare, by all means buy her! And if this bitch doesn't run off and kill Belle the first time she sees steam cars, I'll refund your money. Now, by god, if that's the way things are at your house, go ahead and buy the mare!"

"Three hundred and seventy-five dollars," bid Jim Cromwell, and the mare was knocked down to him. After Uncle Will's fireworks, of course, no one else would make a bid. Needless to say, the mare did not kill Belle Cromwell, but Uncle Will was always sure she would.

One more horse trading story:

Uncle Will was fond of Ike Walker. He had made quite a lot of money in the tobacco business, and had married Uncle Will's niece, Molly Crenshaw. Now Ike wanted to buy a nice horse for Molly to drive. He and his wife were visiting at Wildwood for awhile, and on Sunday afternoon he was with Uncle Will and the other men as they looked over the barns and stock.

"How about that bay filly, the one with the four white ankles?" asked Ike. "She's a beauty!"

"She is that," said Uncle Will, "and she looks to me like the best goddamn filly in Mercer County. She's gentle as a lamb too—worth a lot of money."

"Would you sell her?"

"No, I don't believe so. I think I'll just keep her and show her at the fairs. She'll beat all of them in the fine harness class at Lexington in August."

"I'd like to buy her for Molly. I'll give you $300 for her."

"Ike Walker," stormed Uncle Will, "I've heard you were crazy as hell, and now I know it. The filly's not worth over half that amount. You better go on back to the house before you get cheated."

On one of his frequent trips to Cynthiana, Uncle Will was accompanied by Sarah Eliza. Since she had quietly but firmly refused to go skyrocketing through the country behind Black Joe, they went on the train. Glave had driven them to Burgin where they caught the Southern for Lexington. There they had changed to the L & N for Cynthiana.

The day was hot, and as soon as he sat down Uncle Will reached over Sarah Eliza to raise the window. He couldn't do it with one hand, so he leaned over a little further and got both hands on the window. Still it would not budge. He then had Sarah Eliza move over to the outside of the seat and began to work on the window in earnest. But he couldn't raise it at all. Finally, he told Sarah Eliza to move across the aisle. When she was settled, he lifted up his right foot and kicked the window glass out.

He took off his hat, brushed the glass from the seat, and had Sarah Eliza come back. It did not seem to enter

66

his mind to try another seat where the window might have worked more easily. He wanted that particular seat and he wanted the window up.

He sat down by Sarah Eliza and awaited the arrival of the conductor for the tickets. When Ben McGraw came up, he handed him the tickets plus a five dollar bill. "Ben," he said, "here's $5.00 for that window I broke out because I couldn't get it open. We wanted some air. Kind of stuffy in here."

That was all there was to it. Uncle Will picked up the *Courier-Journal* and proceeded to read Henry Watterson's editorial. He chuckled to himself. Henry Watterson was certainly giving them hell again. There was a newspaper man!

When each of the Goddard boys turned seventeen, Uncle Will gave him a driving horse (usually a colt bred at Wildwood) to break and to have as his own. The boys drove these colts to Harrodsburg, to Danville, and to Lexington; they showed them at the fairs and traded them; sometimes they sold them and bought other horses.

One of their favorite events was the Harrodsburg Fair with its Roadster Rings. The fairgrounds were built around an open circle with a track about an eighth of a mile in circumference immediately on the inside of the enclosure. This track was used to show the horses: the contestants drove their horses around and around it, and the one that showed the most speed, the best "way of going," and stayed best on the trot won the class.

Drivers were spilled, vehicles were upset, wheels were taken off; but all of this was part of the game and added to the fun of the Road Ring. Often a product of Wildwood won. Sometimes Glave or Nick or Reb or Paul or Ralph won with his own horse and, of course, a horse that won in the Roadster class would bring a good price. So it was after winning that the boys were most likely to sell their horses and start in again on a young colt to break and train.

The trip home from the fair was a joy for Uncle Will. Perhaps Gran Cecil was waiting to race him to his gate! Poor Aunt Sally would be hanging frantically to the side of the buggy as Uncle Will kept his horse trotting, trailing behind Gran until they came to a place in the road where it was wide enough for him to pass. Then he'd forge victoriously ahead—unless of course Gran was driving a young Gambetta Wilkes pacer. In those days pacers did not occupy the place assigned to trotters, but they could really go.

After Gran Cecil turned into his gate at Melrose, victorious or vanquished, there was almost always someone else driving further up the road to challenge and race. All it took was the sight of Uncle Will, and immediately, reins would tighten, whips leapt out of their sockets, and the two men would race until one of them turned in at his gate. It was grand!

In the twelve miles from the fairgrounds to Wildwood, Uncle Will would engage in perhaps six or eight races. These races were invariably discussed the next Monday at Harrodsburg Court Day and for many days thereafter.

Court Day in Harrodsburg, in Danville, in Nicholasville, in any county seat in Kentucky, was an important day. On this day the fiscal court met, deeds were recorded, and wills were probated. In Lexington, the farmers congregated to trade their livestock and produce next to the courthouse on Cheapside. Court Day in Danville, the seat of Boyle County, was the third Monday of each month, and there, the farmers would bring their horses, mules, colts, cattle, and hogs to Jockey Row to trade or sell. Story has it that Ben Hardin got the Kentucky State Legislature to create Boyle County from a part of Mercer because he was displeased at some decision handed down by the Mercer County Court. In any case, there were some good people living in Boyle, as far as Uncle Will was concerned: the Boyles, the Rodes, the Cecils, the Hundleys, the Caldwells, the Cowans.

Many horses that Uncle Will passed or did not pass in races on the turnpike he later bought and sold for a fine price. He was always on the lookout for a good gaited, good looking horse with a long neck and a bright eye. Even if the horse was half-starved and bony, Uncle Will's practiced eye could see the horse as he would be a year hence, fattened up and in good coat, ready to be sold.

When he found a promising colt, he had him carefully broken to harness and to saddle and then sent him to some professional trainer to school and show and maybe sell. There was always a market for a good horse in Central Kentucky; in Uncle Will's day a Kentuckian was judged by the horses he drove—and perhaps even more by the horses his wife drove.

Every year a gypsy named Joe came to Mercer and Jessamine counties with his whole band, bringing with them forty or fifty horses to trade to the farmers along the way. Joe was known to all the farmers and horsemen in Central Kentucky. Each winter he'd ship his horses to St. Louis to sell them, and early the next spring he'd buy one or two and just start out swapping as he and the other gypsies of his tribe went on their way.

My father used to see Joe in St. Louis quite often when the gypsy was selling his horses, and he used to tell the story of Joe's transaction with Colonel Early, from North Carolina. That winter Joe had two carloads of about fifty head of horses to sell. He had tried to sell them to everyone, but horses were cheap at that time and the buyers were rather suspicious of Joe anyway. One morning Colonel Early, who was not so particular about quality as he was about price, came to the horse market and Joe approached him.

The market was set up in a barn with a long wooden alley down the middle of it; on either side of the alley there were large pens holding about twenty to twenty-five horses. Joe had two pens. Since the Colonel had seemed willing to look the horses over, Joe fastened the gates at each end of the alley and with much whip cracking drove the horses out of the pens. "How much for all fifty, Joe, take them as they are?"

"One hundred and fifty dollars a head," Joe told him.

"I'll give you fifty dollars apiece," said the Colonel.

"Colonel, you have bought fifty horses."

Joe and Uncle Will traded horses sometimes; however, unless he was in great need, Joe avoided these trades. "Mr. Goddard, he is a sharp man," said Joe. "He is hard to fool."

Although gypsies, various peddlers, and panhandlers came through the country, asking for a couple day's field work along the way, itinerant laborers at that time were rare. So the boys' curiosity was sparked when a man came to Wildwood to ask for a job during wheat harvest one year. Uncle Will hired him and found him to be a good worker, but he was a very quiet man, and uncommunicative about where he came from or why he was in Harrodsburg.

It was apparent that the man was no gypsy. He stayed on around Harrodsburg, mostly at Wildwood, but every so often he would just go away, usually for a week or ten days at a time. The boys, of course, wanted to find out who the stranger was. But Uncle Will told them, "It is none of your damn business. As long as the man does his work, behaves himself, and doesn't drink, he will have a job at Wildwood."

No one visited him; he received no mail; he spoke only when spoken to; and he was polite to the ladies. He told them his name was James Franklin, and except for his unexplained absences, he stayed on for about two years. He'd simply tell Uncle Will that he was going away for awhile and that he'd be back on such and such a day; and he always was. He was a particularly good rider, sat a horse well, and was an excellent judge of a horse. Occasionally he jogged some of the Red Leaf colts, and he seemed to be perfectly at home with the horses.

He left just as suddenly as he'd come. No one knew who he was until years later, when Reb saw this self-same man starting horses at the races in the West. He was the notorious bandit, Frank James, the brother of Jesse.

6

GOOD FRIENDS
AND CLEVER NEIGHBORS

Uncle Will had a keen sense of humor, and he was somewhat of a philosopher, I guess. In any case, he had a great capacity for making friends—and what is more important, a greater capacity for holding them. He was a tireless man, forthright, with a loyalty that could not be swerved. He was as good a judge of people as he was of livestock, and his generosity was proverbial. There was a quality of leadership in him, a fearlessness, and a genuine hatred of sham and pretense. He was certainly prejudiced, as men of his temperament often are, but he was also quick to lend a hand to anyone who needed it. Every tramp, peddler, and panhandler could count on a meal at Wildwood. And Uncle Will's friends were always sure of his affection and his help; after all, he was more prejudiced in favor of his friends than he was against his enemies! It was only natural that Uncle Will should have been looked up to and been very popular in the neighborhood.

Uncle Will had a lot of friends. He liked some of them because of special qualities they possessed. Others he just liked, "but, by god, I don't know why." Conversely, there were people he just naturally did *not* like. Cassius

Clay, Abe Lincoln, and the Devil were all in the same category and just in that order.

Henry Clay had been all right. He was a damn good farmer and stockman as well as a statesman. But John Hunt Morgan—now there was a man to stir the imagination: the great Equestrian, dashing across Kentucky, adored by his men! During the Civil War Uncle Will sent him provisions and did several important jobs for him.

Billy Breckinridge * was an orator beyond compare; Uncle Will never missed a chance to hear him and invite him to Wildwood when he was in or around Harrodsburg.

Later there was Henry Watterson, who made journalistic history as editor of the Louisville *Courier-Journal.* "He's a man who's not afraid to say what he thinks," said Uncle Will, "and by god, I'm not either!" Henry Watterson possessed personal courage and a gift for fury that delighted Uncle Will. They saw eye to eye on nearly everything, except for the subject of whiskey.

Across the road from Wildwood was Leonatus, the home of Captain Jack Chinn. Jack Chinn had won the Kentucky Derby in 1883 with Leonatus and named the farm for the horse. It was this same Jack Chinn who was walking by the side of William Goebel the day he was shot as he was going to his inauguration for Governor of Kentucky. But that was after Uncle Will died.

Jack Chinn drank a little too much whiskey, Uncle Will thought, but he was brave, knowledgeable, and loyal, "a man and a gentleman, by god, a damn good horseman, and a clever neighbor."

An itinerant preacher called one day at Leonatus and found the Captain sitting on his porch with a hound dog at his feet and a shot of whiskey in his hand. Perhaps he had heard that Captain Jack was not much of a churchgoer, for the preacher asked to pray with the family.

* Colonel W. C. P. Breckinridge.

74

But the Captain said, "Now brother, there's no one here except Mrs. Chinn, and she's the best woman that ever lived. In fact, she's a saint, and really doesn't need any praying for. She's taking a nap right now, and she's such a sure bet to get to Heaven that it really wouldn't be any use to disturb her."

"Well, what about you, sir? Don't *you* want to ask the Lord for something? His mercy is boundless and surely you need something from Him," the preacher said earnestly.

"Young man," drawled Captain Jack from his rocking chair, "do you see this house? Do you see this farm extending back to that ash tree? Five hundred acres as good as lies out-of-doors. There are eighty-five short-horn steers in that field to the left and one hundred ewes in that field over there." He indicated them with a sweep of his hand. "The barns are full of feed, and there's a crib of corn for those shoats behind the jack barn. All of it is paid for. The Lord has been so much better to me than I deserve and has taken so much better care of me than I expected that I just wouldn't have the nerve to ask Him for anything else."

Then there were the Thompson neighbors. The Thompsons were distillers, politicians, and lawyers; they were ready at any time for a fight, and to fight one was to fight all. Little Phil was a Congressman and a great friend of Uncle Will. His twin brother had large interests in Washington and ran distilleries in Mercer County as well. When a friend asked him one day how he could spend so much time in Washington and still look after his interests in Harrodsburg, he replied that out of the 4,000 people living in Harrodsburg, there were some 3,999 looking after that business for him!

The Handys, of course, were close neighbors. Some of their relatives lived over in Jessamine County at Handy's Bend, a neck of land of about 2,000 acres on the Kentucky River. Here it was that the two Handy brothers Jim and Tom lived. Somehow or another they had fallen out with each other, and after bitter threats and words, stopped speaking altogether. They had a fence run right down through their property, halving everything, even the house.

Eventually, they grew quite old, and one day Jim became very ill. Uncle Will certainly did not approve of families not speaking, so he decided to go down to Handy's Bend and get Tom to go over to see Jim and shake his brother's hand before he died. At first Tom was obdurate. But Uncle Will pleaded and he swore, and finally, after much persuasion, Tom agreed, reluctantly, to go with him across the fence to shake hands with brother Jim.

Jim was quite weak by this time and didn't look very long for this world. Uncle Will told him what he had done, and Jim feebly raised his hand. Tom came forward. They shook hands. Then Tom said, "Jim, I'm shaking hands and making up with you because I believe you are going to die; but, Jim, if you get well, the whole damn thing's off!" Strange to relate, Jim did get well. He and Tom never spoke to each other again.

The Forsythes also lived near Wildwood; their "Fountain Blue" farm (no doubt a corruption of *Fontainebleau*) was famous for the great thoroughbred horses it sent out to the turf.

Over near Danville in Boyle County, the Cecils were also celebrated horse breeders. Their standardbreds, mostly descendants of Gambetta Wilkes, were internationally famous.

Another friend to Uncle Will was Governor McCreary. He was twice Governor and United States Senator; the last county to be named in Kentucky was named for him. When McCreary headed the Democratic ticket for Governor, he had asked Uncle Will to make the race for a state office. But to all his pleadings Uncle Will turned a deaf ear. "I'll be hell for you though," he said. And he was.

Uncle Will also took the privilege of being hell *against*

a candidate when the situation seemed to warrant it. One year, a man whom my grandfather particularly disliked was running in the state senator's race. And if John Berry disliked a man, by god, so did W. W. Goddard! Uncle Will actually took the stump against him. He had heard that this man was so stingy that he gave his children a dime not to eat supper and then took the money away from them after they had gone to bed. Uncle Will was so furious that he wanted to horsewhip him. In fact, although they had never met, when he ran into the man on the street in Harrodsburg, Uncle Will told him what he thought of him and, furthermore, said never to speak to him or any of his family. "If you do, I'll give you the goddamnest thrashing you ever had," he said. As it turned out, the man was badly beaten in the primary and moved away. Good riddance of bad rubbish! Uncle Will did not like to associate with such trash. "If you lie down with dogs, you'll get up with fleas," he'd say—and he'd say it often.

Uncle Will's friends were generally people who had the happy faculty for gracious, yet at times strenuous living. These were the people who visited Wildwood on Sunday afternoons. These were the people whose horses you saw at the county fairs and race meetings, whose chickens you fought in the tobacco barn.

Fighting chickens held a fascination for Uncle Will; the excitement, the quick action, and above all the courage of the cocks appealed to him. Whenever there was a main, he was usually there. Gabe Jackson, the man who tended the tollgate, used to fight chickens every night—he had trained the Wildwood chickens, and they were good ones: Doms, marked like Barred Rocks, and known for their courage and stamina. The Arkansas Travelers were quick fighters all right, but the Doms "stayed in fighting to the last and could take it."

A man would come to the fight with a number of chickens, pay an entry fee, and have his stags weighed in. Fights were staged according to weight, and an odd-numbered series of these fights constituted a main. The owner whose chickens won the most fights took the prize money for the main.

Betting was fast. "I bet $50.00 on the Round Head." "A hundred dollars on the Syd Taylor Cock." A finger raised in the crowd meant the bet was taken. That's all. There was never any welching either! After the cock had been declared the winner, the losing bettor came right over and paid off.

Chicken fights were real community events; in some counties they involved wives and children who brought picnic baskets and sat on the lawn while the men fought their stags. Outsiders were admitted to the main, but could only participate in so-called hack fights, their chickens pitted against those of another outsider.

After all, the fights were a matter of neighborhood status and pride—if a cock was a poor fighter, or more rarely, tried to get out of the pit away from the fighting the owner was deeply humiliated. The game required speed, action, and sportsmanship in good measure.

All in all the neighborhood atmosphere was pretty congenial, if somewhat tense from time to time, but through it all, Uncle Will was *always* in a hell of a hurry. He was never abashed, and never afraid to speak his piece and "let the chips fall where they may." He was at home in any assembly of notables because he himself was one of them, a great man.

Uncle Will always considered and took an interest in the tenants and hands on the farm. Tenants usually raised about five acres of tobacco and sometimes eight or ten acres of corn on a fifty-fifty basis. Uncle Will would make sure that the tenants' wives and children were included in all the big parties given at Wildwood. Today there are a number of landowners in Kentucky whose fathers or grandfathers were tenants for such men as Will Goddard, Jack Chinn, Fred Forsythe, or George Handy.

Pat Frazer and Tom Hoover, also neighbors of Uncle Will, lived across the road from each other and were boon companions. Pat had gone to California in 1849 with James Ben Ali Haggin. Mr. Haggin went on to be successful; Mr. Frazer came back home. Now he and Tom often sat nights in the back of Tom's store, taking a few drinks and discussing the topics of the day.

One night the conversation got around to a discussion of the Bible, and the two friends decided to read it. Neither one of them knowing much about the Bible in general, they entered upon a contest to see which of them could read it through first. Every night over the ever-present jug they would compare progress and discuss what they had read.

As it happened, Pat finished first, and that night he came over mighty well satisfied with himself. Tom brought the jug out and poured the whiskey, and finally he asked, "Well Pat, just what did you think of it?"

"Well, I tell you Tom," he said, shaking his head, "it's a passel of scandal from kiver to kiver."

Ben Gratz of Lexington, another of Uncle Will's friends, was a good deal like the squire of Wildwood himself. Story has it that when Mr. Gratz asked an acquaintance how he was feeling that morning, the man replied, "Well, to tell you the truth, Mr. Gratz, I am a sick man. My liver is out of order; I have rheumatism so bad that I can hardly move." As a matter of fact, the man had *everything* the matter with him, and he went into glowing anatomical descriptions to boot. As he paused for breath, Mr. Gratz said, "Shut up, damn it, I really don't care how you are; I only asked you for politeness' sake."

One time Mr. Gratz borrowed a dress suit from his friend Ed DeLong and did not return it for many weeks. Finally, Mr. DeLong met Mr. Gratz unexpectedly, and decided to ask him for the suit. Apologetically he explained that his daughter Kate was to be married and that he would need the suit on that occasion. Mr. Gratz replied, "Ed, I'm sorry, but I can't let you have that dress suit. What in hell do you think *I'm* going to wear? I'm going to that wedding too."

Colonel Dick Redd was about the last of the Confederate veterans. Right up until his death he rode a horse and led all of the parades through the streets of Lexington. Upon every possible occasion he wore his Confederate uniform and gave the Rebel yell. I can still remember him dancing before the Lord on the Sunday his youngest niece was baptized at the First Pesbyterian Church in Lexington. He always claimed the Union survivors were few in number and a bunch of softies. He had outlived them all. "Look at me!" he'd exclaim. "Look at me, hail and hearty. The G.A.R's all got pensions, lived high, and died of gout. The Confederate veterans had to live off of corn bread and buttermilk, and look at us, still going strong!"

Uncle Will counted many political leaders of the county, state, and nation among his friends. However, he would never run for office, although personal bias leads me to believe that he could have had almost any state office he wanted. He was always a Democrat; but he didn't always support the popular candidate or the so-called organization candidate either.

When a candidate asked him for his support, Uncle Will would tell him, "I'll let you know in a day or two, and if I'm for you, I'll be hell for you, and if I'm against you, I'll be hell against you." And he'd let him know just as readily if he was against him as he would if he were for him.

Many of the great and the near-great were entertained at Wildwood, and many of them Uncle Will considered warm friends, but none held the place of respect that was reserved for William Jennings Bryan.

Uncle Will was also very close to James B. Beck, who, had he been born in the United States, might well have stepped from the United States Senate into the Presidency. On one of his trips to New York, Senator Beck sent Uncle Will a shaving mug, which the Master of Wildwood used until his death.

John G. Carlisle was a frequent visitor at Wildwood; and Joe C. Blackburn, United States Senator from Versailles, Kentucky, always had a slight repast at Wildwood whenever he was in that vicinity. The "slight repast" served at Wildwood consisted of at least three kinds of meat, not less than six vegetables, myriads of jellies, preserves, and pickles, several salads, three desserts, and two or three kinds of cake. The reports of these "slight repasts" spread far beyond the confines of Mercer County.

Uncle Will was present at all Democratic speakings. If he was "hell for" the candidate, he would be on the speakers' platform. If he was "hell against" him he would be in the audience and generally asked a few questions that the candidate found embarrassing to answer.

Quite a discussion arose in Harrodsburg at one time about running the railroad into town. Uncle Will was opposed to it—and in the minority. But against it he was. The goddamned engines were always scaring his horses. Besides that, Burgin, where the main line of the Southern ran, was only three miles away. The railroad they were planning on putting into Harrodsburg was only a branch. Moreover, Uncle Will didn't like the way this railroad had played politics and done some unsavory things in Frankfort.

A big mass meeting was held one night to put the idea over to the populace, get some right of ways deeded, and perhaps collect a few dollars into the bargain.

The meeting started, and many people expressed their approval of the plan; but General Bennett H. Young of Louisville was there to make the real plea. Uncle Will listened intently as the General spoke. He was painting the benefits of the new railroad in glowing colors: in addition to the educational advantages to be had thereof, the railroad would be an easy way to get cattle, tobacco, and other products to the larger market in Louisville; it would be an easier—and cheaper—way to get needed commodities to Harrodsburg.

"And your coal!" he exclaimed, "the coal for which you are now paying six cents a bushel! When the railroad comes in, you will be able to buy it for *one cent* per bushel!" The General beamed upon his audience, letting his words take their effect.

At once Uncle Will got up from his seat in the rear of the hall and started down the aisle. He had his glasses on and he was taking his wallet out of his hip pocket. "General Young, by god, I want 500,000 bushels of coal, and here's the money for it. And furthermore, at that price, I'll sell Wildwood and put it *all* in coal!"

The audience chuckled and nudged one another; Mr. Goddard had done it again. The General cleared his throat once or twice. "Perhaps I did put the figure a little too low, Mr. Goddard; I stand corrected. Three cents per bushel."

"All right, by god, then three cents per bushel; I want 500,000 delivered to Harrodsburg, and here's the money." By this time Uncle Will was on the platform, thrusting the money into the nonplussed General's face.

Finally, the General had to admit that he was entirely wrong in his estimate. Uncle Will walked out, still flourishing the money and swearing that he wanted the 500,000 bushels of coal. After Uncle Will's exit there was nothing to do but to declare the meeting adjourned. Uncle Will had closed it up, and no more was to be said on the subject that night.

7

THIS YEAR — THE BEATEN BISCUITS

Weeks before the Harrodsburg Fair, which was held around the first of August, Uncle Will saw to it that all Wildwood was in a ferment of excitement getting ready to participate in a big way. Uncle Will had helped to organize the fair at Harrodsburg in 1870, and since that date, each year he was one of its most enthusiastic promoters and exhibitors.

In fact the morning after the fair was over, when Uncle Will was making his daily tour of the farm, he was already planning his livestock, crop, and garden entries for the next year's fair. By the middle of June he had managed to arouse the whole household at Wildwood so that the members of the family and the various hands on the place were in a state of feverish participation.

Horses, shorthorn cattle, Southdown sheep, and hogs were specially fed and curried and sleeked down so that they'd bring home in triumph many blue ribbons and a suitable number of grand champion purples. Hemp, corn, wheat, and tobacco that had grown properly were set aside for display.

Watermelons of prodigious size were taken off the vines at the exact moment of perfection and removed to the springhouse for safekeeping. The best bunches of grapes were covered with bags to protect them from insects. Apples, peaches, pears, and plums were selected from the orchard. Tomatoes, eggplants, cucumbers, beans, okra, and any other vegetables that were unusually large and well formed were also reserved for showing at the fair.

On the Monday before the opening day of the fair, the kitchen was such a beehive of activity that it delighted Uncle Will's heart. Jellies, preserves, and pickles were put up in glass containers that had held prizewinning condiments at past fairs. Cakes, pies, loaves of salt-rising bread, light rolls, beaten biscuits, and candy were turned out in great array. Several times during the day he'd pass by the kitchen door on his way to the barns or fields and shout a few words of encouragement.

Ina and Rea in the late '80s were too young to be considered young ladies, although Ina was beginning to be "set out"; but even so, Ina had won the blue ribbon every year for four years on her angel food cake, and Rea had won last year on her marble cake. Sister Mamie, the oldest daughter, always won with salt-rising bread and Sally Lunn. This year some member of the family would have to manage to get the blue ribbon on beaten biscuits.

Kizzie, the cook, stirred the cake batter and kneaded the dough, directed by the young ladies. Her children, Willy, aged sixteen, and Sally, aged fourteen, named for "Marse Will" and "Miz Sarah Liza," fetched spices and flour and sugar and butter and even took turns stirring and beating when Kizzie was busy testing the oven or taking out the cakes. Little Ina Rea, who was six years old, ran errands, and Martha, the housemaid, was called in to lend a hand.

"Where are Ned and Silas?" Mamie would ask. "We need them to bring up the stone jars of pickled peaches and relish from the cellar."

"Now you know Miss Mamie," Kizzie would tell her,

"those two boys haven't been near this house for two-three weeks. We'se lucky to have Willy here. Marse Will's got everybody out to the stable looking after the horses and cattle."

Spread out on the spare room bed were freshly laundered or newly pressed fancywork to be sent to Floral Hall. There were quilts, pillow shams, knitted counterpanes, embroidered and hand-drawn tablecloths and center pieces, and crocheted afghans and antimacassars.

In the flower garden, Aunt Sally and Ina had watered the dahlias, verbenas, zinnias, and phlox, and hoped that the August lilies would bloom in time. The huge lemon verbenas, crepe myrtles, oleanders, and pomegranates in tubs in front of the house would all furnish bouquets for the flower show, and perhaps the cape jasmines might have a blossom or two by then.

The Harrodsburg Fair also meant a house full of company at Wildwood. Each of the five older children would have from one to three guests apiece, and Uncle Will would bring home with him as many of his cronies as he could corral at the fair. There was a dance every night, and huge picnic lunches had to be prepared for the four days. The Harrodsburg Fair was a gala occasion, so gala and so strenuous that a less hearty generation might have seasoned the dish of anticipated joys with the salt of reasonable foreknowledge of weariness.

Imagine the consternation that greeted Sister Mamie's report upon her return from the garden the Monday morning before the fair that the zinnias and dahlias and verbenas had all been eaten off, and the August lilies were trampled to pieces!

"It's the Animal that did it," moaned Ina. "The Animal got out of its yard last night, and the men caught it in the garden. It couldn't have been in there more than a few minutes! Mama," she cried, "did you hear that the Animal ruined all the flowers in the garden?"

Ina and her mother comforted each other as best they could, because in truth, the bull, King of Sharon, the

crowning pride of Unce Will's shorthorn herd, had devastated the garden during his brief sojourn there. Never, never, among the ladies was King of Sharon referred to as the bull. Such designation was indelicate, actually *indecent*. The bull was "the Animal" and "the Animal" was never "he" but "it."

The day of the fair arrived, a perfect day of golden sunshine and blue sky. At breakfast Uncle Will announced that all four days would be without rain; every sign pointed to the best weather possible, and the best possible fair. The fancywork, garden, and farm produce had been taken to Floral Hall on Tuesday afternoon, and the girls had decorated Reb's high wheeled, no-top buggy for the Fancy Turnout Ring. They had covered it with large yellow and white chrysanthemums, and Reb was going to drive the Red Leaf colt with reins of yellow and white satin ribbon.

Uncle Will had been up most of the night to see that his sons, Glave, Nicholas, Rebel, Paul, Ralph, and even little Will, along with the Negroes and the tenant farmers and their sons, got the livestock on the way to the fairgrounds during the night so that the horses, cattle, sheep, and hogs would all arrive in the cool of the morning and be comfortable in their stalls and pens before the sun was on them.

The cakes and jellies and other foods had to be at Floral Hall by 9 o'clock, when the judging began.

Breakfast was at 6 o'clock as usual. Sarah Eliza, Sister Lizzie, the three girls, and their six visitors were at the table when Uncle Will came in from his daily tour of the farm.

Uncle Will had made a rule that no matter what hour one had retired after a late ball, or upon arrival from a trip, *everybody* at Wildwood had to appear at breakfast on time and fully clad.

"You can go back to bed if you want to and sleep all day; but you've got to be at breakfast on time. And I won't have any damned dressing sacks and Mother

Hubbards at the table!" Uncle Will explained this often enough for the rule to be remembered. But no rule had been needed this morning to see that all the household was to breakfast on time.

Uncle Will was in a regular "swidget." He gave directions to everybody and made plans for everything.

"Sarah Eliza, Silas will drive you and Sister Lizzie and two of the girls in the surrey. Mamie, you drive two of the girls in the buggy with you. Ina, you and Rea come in the carriage with two girls and let Willy drive you. Ned is here to hitch up the horses for you when you want to start. Give yourselves plenty of time now, and don't drive too fast. Ned and Kizzie and Martha can come in the spring wagon with the damned preserves and cake and pickles! We should better eat them today than show them. Have you got enough for dinner for everybody? Don't forget the watermelons in the springhouse. Let 'em stay till the last minute to keep 'em cool!"

Uncle Will covered everything—the management of the exhibits, the hour for dinner to be spread under the big oak tree south of the show ring, every possible detail of arrangement. And Sarah Eliza never argued with him of course; in the end she did as she thought best.

As Uncle Will swung out of sight on Black Joe at a fast gallop he was still yelling back directions. "See you at 12 o'clock under the big oak tree!"

This particular fair was in 1889, and it was of special interest because Nancy Hanks, already showing signs of becoming a champion, was to start in the three-year-old trotting race that afternoon. Among the other horses racing against her was Bonnie Wilmore, bred in Boyle County and owned in Harrodsburg. This colt was highly thought of, and there was much speculation on the race. When Bonnie Wilmore won the first heat, with Abbie V second, and Nancy Hanks third, the crowd went wild. It was all over. "Bonnie Wilmore is a great colt! Even the skill of Ben Kenny can't make Nancy Hanks win!" the crowd exclaimed. But Nancy Hanks did win the next *three* heats and never lost another heat in her racing career. She became a world's champion racing mare and a world champion broodmare.

In fact, the trotter Nancy Hanks became so famous in Central Kentucky that when she died she was enshrined in a horse cemetery on Hamburg Place near Lexington. Many years later some ardent Daughters of America, bearing a wreath, asked to be directed to the grave of Nancy Hanks. They were told to go out four miles on the Winchester Pike and the grave would be on the right hand side of the road. The Daughters returned to Lexington storming with indignation. "We bought the wreath for Nancy Hanks, the mother of Lincoln," they exploded, "and we found the grave of a horse!"

The mother of Lincoln is buried in Indiana. Moreover, no Kentuckian sees any incongruity about placing a wreath on the grave of a horse.

At 12 o'clock the Wildwood crowd were all assembled under the big oak tree—Uncle Will, Aunt Sally, Sister Lizzie and Brother Ed Glave, the three Goddard young ladies and their six visitors, and the six Goddard boys and their three house guests. Uncle Will had brought Jim Cromwell, Temple Withers, the Shropshire boys, Bob Berry, Major Thomas, and several other friends with him. From time to time Harrodsburg swains came by for a word or two with Mamie or Ina or Rea or some of the guests, and all partook of the salad, old ham, stuffed eggs, ice cream, cake, or watermelon, depending much upon the part of the feast during which they had arrived.

One of the young men who came by was from New York, and Ina was pointing out to him the various people of interest. As some unusually large young ladies strolled by she said, "There go Laura and Jane Finley. Their father has a thousand acres of Bluegrass land." Whereupon the young man asked, "Do you think those Finley girls ate all of those acres?"

At the picnic dinner the girls sat on cushions, the toes of their shoes barely peeping from under their ruffled skirts, and the boys sat on the grass near them. Uncle Will and his friends discussed livestock, earlier fairs, and events of the day. Aunt Sally sat on the surrey seat that had been put on the ground for her and directed the activities without seeming to give any orders at all.

Kizzie, Ned, Silas, Martha, Willy, Sally, and Ina Rea passed mountains of fried chicken, huge platters of old ham and spring lamb, dozens of stuffed eggs, mounds of cottage cheese, chicken salad and slaw, along with buttered slices of homemade light bread, beaten biscuits, watermelon pickles, stuffed cucumber pickles, damson preserves, blackberry jelly, red raspberry and currant jam, and individual apple and custard pies. The two-gallon freezer of ice cream was then opened and everyone had enormous helpings of homemade vanilla ice cream, slices of white pound cake, and spice jam cake. Uncle Will insisted too that they top off the dinner with three-inch-thick rounds of the "best goddamned watermelon you ever ate."

After dinner the girls and boys walked around the fairgrounds. Aunt Sally and her sister-in-law found seats in the grandstand. The men went to the barns to inspect their livestock and then to the show ring or to the grandstand. Later the boys would show the horses and cattle. Rea, the youngest daughter, was riding this year in the Girls' Riding Class. Mamie was to drive with Bob Curry in the Fine Harness Ring, and Rebel had asked Bird Martin to drive in the Fancy Turnout Ring with him. The other young ladies were hoping that they too would be asked by some of the local gallants to drive in some of the rings before the day was over.

Meanwhile, some of the swains had slipped off to the hootchy-kootchy show, which was always placed conveniently near the cattle barns. The young men could thus come out of the back of the show, walk through the cattle barns, and saunter into the grandstand. In those days, such breathtaking exhibitions took the place of the striptease.

Ice cream cones had not yet been invented, but pink lemonade was sold. There was also a "beer garden" on the fairgrounds, with high canvas around it and a wicked look about it. Uncle Will saw to it that no beer was actually sold in the "beer garden" at the Harrodsburg Fair; however, it was not a place for respectable young ladies, and it was worth any female reputation to be seen in one. The hootchy-kootchy show she must not even mention!

The merry-go-round, a novelty indeed in the late '80s, was part of the fair that year. Soon young people were flocking to this carousel, the Goddard house party among them. The young ladies and their beaux sat decorously in the sleighs, while the young men unaccompanied by the damsels rode on the horses, the zebras, the lions, and the tigers.

After awhile, Lizzie Berry and Asa Jewell became tired of the sleighs; so finally Lizzie grew bold and mounted one of the horses. She sat as if she were on a sidesaddle, facing the calliope, her skirts pulled down well over her ankles to the tips of her shoes. Asa rode the other horse beside her. How smart and daring Lizzie was, he thought to himself, riding the horse because she wanted to even though she knew she was being unconventional. She had been careful to be modest sitting that way, and she certainly did have a pretty figure!

Uncle Will was in the ring with his shorthorn cattle and his Sumpter Denmark colts. They had behaved quite satisfactorily and won a number of prizes. He cherished those ribbons, and the recognition was more than enough for him; but it was winning the coin silver goblets, julep cups, teaspoons, and silver pitchers that Sarah Eliza and the girls set such great store by. He recalled seeing Reb drive off behind the Red Leaf colt with a blue ribbon himself. Now the trotting races, the final events of the day, were beginning. So Uncle Will went to the grandstand with Jim Cromwell, General Withers, Major Thomas, and others to watch.

As they entered the grandstand, they recognized one of Uncle Will's neighbors, Jim Eastland, whose Turner K was in the next race. This was the first time Jim had ever had a horse in a race and he was so excited that he was nearly beside himself. Uncle Will asked about his horse, and they all wished him well in the race. Crit Davis, a potent trotting horse man, considered by many to be one of the world's greatest race drivers, was driving the horse.

After some attempts and false starts when the trotters were called back once or twice, the starter said "Go!" and the horses were off. Immediately, Jim Eastland began to wring his hands and sob, "Oh! Mr. Davis, don't let him break! Oh! Mr. Goddard, do you think he'll stay on a trot? Oh! Mr. Davis, don't let him break! Oh! Mr. Goddard, do you think he'll stay on a trot? Oh! Turner K, please don't break! Please keep trotting! Mr. Goddard, I couldn't stand it if he broke!"

This continued until the horses turned into the home stretch. Jim was wringing his hands frantically and nearly in tears. Uncle Will could stand such goings on no longer. He turned on the young man, shook him fiercely, and said, "Goddamn it, young man, keep quiet! It's all part of the game!"

When the races were over, Uncle Will and Black Joe were home at Wildwood long before any of the others. He rode over the whole place, put up his horse, and came around the house just in time to help Sarah Eliza, Sister Lizzie, and the young ladies out of the surrey when they drove up the avenue to the stone stoop before the house. The fair was over and there was much work to be done!

I can still remember a hot, blue August day in the mid-'90s when Uncle Will came up from Harrodsburg to Lexington to attend the Blue Grass Fair. He was a little chagrined to have had to come by train, for although he was past seventy-five now, he much preferred driving in his buckboard the thirty-two miles between Wildwood and Lexington. At one time he had kept a horse at my father's farm, halfway between home and town, to change on his way; during Fair time, he'd pick my father up in the buckboard and they'd both ride into Lexington together.

Now at Fair time it was more convenient for our family to stay in town at our Ashland Avenue home, so when Uncle Will arrived at the station, my father would meet him and bring him home for mid-day dinner before going out to the fairgrounds.

I was about six years old then, a "wise child," and apparently unafraid as yet of my tempestuous great great-uncle. Mother overheard our conversation; otherwise, I'm sure that by now it would have long since gone out of my memory.

"Who the hell are in those pictures?" Uncle Will asked as he inspected the pictures on the walls. "Who's this baby?"

"That's Baby Stuart," I answered.

"Well, I'll declare. Jeb Stuart's baby! Jeb was a grand Confederate general. I'm glad to see your mother honors him by having his baby's picture. Who's this sissy little boy all dressed up like a fool?"

"Uncle Will, that's me as Lafayette in a school play last month. They are the most comfortable clothes I ever wore."

"Well, if your mother dresses you up in clothes like that, she's to blame if you turn out wrong. Who's this baby in his mother's lap?"

"That's God and God's mother," I explained of the Madonna of the Chair.

"What are these two pictures?"

"That's a church in Italy, and that's a lake way off somewhere."

Uncle Will sputtered and fumed: "All these pictures

and not a damned one of any kinfolks except that sissy picture of you, and not a Confederate general in the lot. Where's your mother anyway? Lizzie," he called, "come here!"

As Mother came to the door, he burst out: "What do you want these pictures for? Nobody you've ever seen! No place you've ever been! Where's the picture of Morgan's Men your Uncle Bob gave you? Where's your Robert E. Lee? I thought you had one of those enlarged pictures of Sister Evalina. My pictures at home have got some sense to them, but these pictures! Of all the silly, high falutin' nonsense! What in hell do you want to have them around for?"

My father loved to go to the fairs with Uncle Will— there was never a dull moment when he was around— and he loved to talk about those years when Uncle Will was still driving his buckboard into Lexington to attend them. He'd often tell us about the Fair they attended when Uncle Will was seventy-two.

Uncle Will did not feel those seventy-odd years, did not look them, still carried them lightly, and was in just as much of a hurry as he had been some thirty years before when he bought Wildwood. Wildwood had flourished since then, and the nine children with whom Sarah Eliza had presented him were surely the best in the country. On this August morning Uncle Will felt pretty well satisfied with himself.

He wished sometimes that he might take a little time off to watch things, perhaps—the sun coming out from behind the Kentucky River cliffs, the honey-colored light on the maples, the purple haze over High Bridge; to gaze awhile at the shorthorn cattle in the flush of their growth and coat; to inspect the tobacco along the way. But even now he had no time to contemplate. He was in a hell of a hurry and he had to be in Lexington by noon.

My father would rather have driven his own horse to Lexington in safety, but he was unwilling to offend Uncle Will. So he went with him, holding to the side of the buggy while Uncle Will, standing up in the buckboard, urged his horse on.

It was a lovely country they traversed. Past Bird Bryan's large red brick house with the white Corinthian columns; Bird was a near relative of Mrs. Daniel Boone, but more important in Uncle Will's eyes, he was one of Kentucky's best cattle breeders.

Past Joe Patterson's, whose son Willie had driven Kentucky Central a few years before to break the world's record for four-year-old trotters. Mr. Patterson had his own track and trained his own horses. On the day Kentucky Central won his great race, he said, "The way to beat this trotting horse game is to raise and train your own horses and your own drivers."

Then past Jim Guyn's; he was a fine farmer, but a bit on the stingy side, Uncle Will thought.

Sam Barclay's was next; he was probably the best

farmer of them all—not a stockman like Uncle Will; strictly a crop farmer.

Past the Knight farm where years later the three greatest horses from one farm were foaled: Exterminator, Peter Volo, and later, Greyhound.

All through the trip Uncle Will carried on a lively conversation. So and so had been a Union sympathizer; this one drank too much; that one was a Republican; and so on.

They drove into the livery stable near the fairgrounds, where the Sally Wilkes colt was unhitched to rest until Uncle Will started back to Wildwood.

Uncle Will was filled with anticipation; at this time the Fair was in its heyday. The best tobacco would be exhibited here; the finest hemp; the most abundant corn; and the grandest livestock, sheep, and cattle to be found in the world. At Wildwood he was sure that he had the best saddle horses, shorthorn cattle, and Southdown sheep to be seen anywhere; today he would see some of the same blood lines, and they would win all the blue ribbons.

The Shropshires, the Renicks, the Van Meters would all be showing, and these were names to contend with among shorthorn breeders. Abe Renick would be entering his Rose of Sharons, Ben Van Meter his Bates Cattle, and the Shropshire boys would be trying to show a heifer as good as their Fanny Forrester.

"And they are the best goddamn shorthorn cattle in the world," said Uncle Will, "except some I've bred at Wildwood."

Uncle Will expected to see little Jim Graves show Chester Dare in the saddle horse ring that hot summer day. And surely W. H. Wilson would be there with Lady de Jarnette.

"That was a sight I'll never forget," Uncle Will said to my father, "Lizzie Nichols riding Lady de Jarnette at the Cynthiana Fair! Too bad you didn't see them, Asa; a damned handsome pair they made. Lizzie Nichols had on a white riding suit, the side saddle was white, the reins were white, and that Lady de Jarnette, well, she's one of the best goddamned combined saddle mares ever bred!" Lizzie Nichols was kin to Jim Cromwell; he would be here today too with one or more good horses. He was a man after Uncle Will's own heart, Jim Cromwell, and kind of kin folks too. He clapped almost as loudly as Uncle Will when the band played *Dixie*, and he certainly did hate a damyankee. He also knew a fine horse when he saw one.

Uncle Will didn't think very much of Jim's Harrison Chief, however. That stallion was a good harness horse with a lot of speed from his trotting ancestry, but his neck was too short and he just wasn't quite enough horse. You couldn't depend on that bay to make a great sire. He certainly wasn't in the same class as the Denmarks of Wildwood, Uncle Will believed, and would never be the horse that Sumpter Denmark was.

Alas for Uncle Will's prophecy! Harrison Chief, a famous harness and saddle horse, was one of the greatest stallions of all time and a mighty foundation of the saddle horse breed.

As they approached the show ring on this hot August afternoon in the early '90s, Uncle Will and Father were talking of cattle and horses and friends. Uncle Will wanted very much to stop by Floral Hall to see if Sarah Eliza's quilt had won again, but he had to get to the track to see that suckling colt by Sumpter Denmark.

Just past Floral Hall, a tall well-built man approached Uncle Will and held out his hand. "How are you, Mr. Goddard?"

Uncle Will stopped abruptly and dropped his buggy whip. He reached for his spectacles and slowly drew the silver-rimmed glasses from the case. At seventy-two, Uncle Will still did not wear glasses all the time, but when he wished to inspect anybody or anything closely he always put on his spectacles. Now he took out his

98

handkerchief, breathed on the lenses, and wiped them very carefuly. All through the operation he never took his eyes off the man. Slowly, he put on his glasses.

In fact, he was so deliberate about what he was doing that my father began to sense that something was wrong. Uncle Will was never deliberate about anything. He was a stocky, broad-shouldered, fierce little man who moved quickly, suddenly. After he had adjusted his glasses, Uncle Will began to walk slowly around the man, eyeing him closely. Finally, when he had walked completely around him, he came to a stop in front of him. He took his glasses off, carefully put them back in their case, deposited them in his pocket—and let go with a good right to the man's chin! He might have been twenty-seven instead of his seventy-two years. The man went down like one of Uncle Will's shorthorn steers when it was hit in the head with an axe.

"You son of a bitch," he said, "I told you twenty years ago never to speak to me again as long as you lived. You see I am a man of my word." Then, looking neither to the right nor the left, Uncle Will picked up his buggy whip and proceeded to the grandstand.

As he went into the grandstand to watch the trotting races, he saw his friends Major Barak Thomas and General Temple Withers—Major Thomas was the owner of the fleet Himyar and General Withers owned Pilot Medium, the grey crippled horse that sired Peter the Great. Although all of them knew a good horse when they saw one, none of the three could then foresee the tremendous influence that the grey cripple would have on harness horse history through his marvelous son.

It was a fine Fair, and Uncle Will had a wonderful time. Fanny Forrester, later sold for $10,000, looked as well as she had a year ago. It was remarkable how she kept her "bloom." The Sumpter Denmark colt had won. A damned presumptuous fellow had been put in his place. Asa Jewell owed him a hat on the trotting race. And, yes, that quilt of Sarah Eliza had been declared the best in the whole Floral Hall. Uncle Will was secretly proud of that quilt; it made him a little more sure that the best of everything was at Wildwood.

So he was feeling pretty good as he went to the livery stable to have the Sally Wilkes colt hitched to the buckboard. He couldn't possibly spend the night at Pleasant View, he said to my father. He was in a hell of a hurry to get home to put those goddamn hands to work early in the morning; they had probably been loafing all day today. He'd stop twice: once at Cap May's for some sugar and coffee, and again, to change horses at the farm. Then, with Black Joe to the buckboard he'd go on home in a dead run. No driver would pass him on the turnpike; Uncle Will believed in *speed!*

And so Uncle Will proceeded on his way to Wildwood, content with his life, the wife that he adored, his nine fine children. It was a good time to be alive; he was a good farmer, a leader in his community, a successful man. He'd gladly have gone on forever, driving his buckboard, raising his shorthorns, hating the damyankees, deploring lies and whiskey drinking—but right now, as always, he was in a hell of a hurry!